By Alden Todd

ABANDONED: The Story of the Greely Arctic Expedition
JUSTICE ON TRIAL: The Case of Louis D. Brandeis
A SPARK LIGHTED IN PORTLAND
RICHARD MONTGOMERY, REBEL OF 1775
FAVORITE SUBJECTS IN WESTERN ART
    (with Dorothy B. Weisbord)

Finding
Facts Fast

Second Edition

Finding Facts Fast

How to Find Out What You Want and Need to Know

Alden Todd

A handbook for students, political activists, civic leaders and professionals ... based on methods used by reference librarians, scholars, investigative reporters and detectives

TEN SPEED PRESS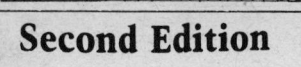

ISBN 0-89815-012-4 paper
ISBN 0-89815-013-2 cloth

Printed in The United States of America.

*To all of you who kindly helped
or patiently listened –
and most of all to Jean,
Paul and Flip.*

Contents

Author to Reader

Finding Facts Fast is for Everyman — for all of you who do research in business, the professions, volunteer committees and politics. It is for secretaries with ambition to move up from typing and filing to executive assistant. It is for students at all levels.

This is a practical and sometimes irreverent book. You can learn from it how to find out what you want to know, with speed and accuracy. You can learn to avoid the time-wasting, needle-in-haystack methods by which most people search for information.

What is new about *Finding Facts Fast*? There are other books with the word "research" on the cover. Most of them are either lists of reference books, arranged by subject, or handbooks that tell a student how to gather material for a paper or thesis, and how to write it. Such books are all right as far as they go, but they are narrowly oriented toward writing term papers and theses. They approach research as something for the student only — done largely in the library. They disregard many practical needs for research skill in daily living. And they do not mention many sources of information outside the library.

Their worst fault is that they place little or no value on a person's time. In the working world where we earn our living, time is money. Very few professors are concerned with this cardinal fact of life when they assign research projects to their students. As a result, graduates emerge from the universities by the thousands with little or no knowledge of the *fast* way to find things out — either in their field of academic specialty or elsewhere. *Finding*

Facts Fast, as its title suggests, is designed to help you learn research techniques that are the fastest, as well as the best and most thorough.

The heart of this book is the methods of thought — the approaches to fact-finding — that it offers. I do not propose to ask the reader to become a walking encyclopedia of memorized sources of information, even though many such sources are to be found here. With practice any intelligent person can master the research methods appropriate to his immediate purpose or line of work, without memorizing things that he can look up easily.

In this book I have adopted the convention of referring to researchers as "he" and librarians as "she," only to avoid tripping over my pronouns in discussion of relations between them. It might have been the other way around, because I know that both men and women do research and serve as reference librarians. No stereotyping is intended.

Finding Facts Fast grew from my own experience, including nine years of research in the Library of Congress, where I wrote books and magazine articles for a living. While there, I was challenged by the richness of the collections around me to learn how best to exploit them. I began to question reference librarians, scholars and (outside the Library) other professional writers, seeking the most efficient research methods. Today I still keep on with this search.

One result of my inquiry has been a course in Research Techniques and Fact-Finding, which I have taught at New York University since 1966. This book is the other.

A.T.

I. About This Book, and Research in General

Your Approach to Research

As in learning anything worthwhile, you should proceed at your own pace in learning research techniques. It does not matter whether you start in high school, in college, as a doctoral degree candidate, or in business, professional or public life when you are years away from formal schooling. Take these pages step by step, with self-confidence but without careless overconfidence.

Examine the reference sources mentioned here; you will be surprised at what you find out about the way in which reference books are organized or indexed, and at what they contain. New editions of reference sources you have used before may contain additional information or features that make them more useful than they used to be.

Don't think you can remember everything; take notes on new information and put them where you can find them later.

Be specific rather than general in inquiries and note-taking, or you may find that you must do the job over again.

Never hesitate to ask for information; the person who knows is usually glad to tell you, and respects you for wanting to learn.

Cultivate persistence in research; the most common failure is to give up too soon.

Above all, enjoy the adventure of searching in order to find out; achieving knowledge is among the deepest of civilized pleasures.

You Have to Practice

Right at the start, face the fact that reading this book, even studying it, is not enough. To become a good research worker you have to practice. The reader should study the methods of research described in this book. Then, if he is serious about acquiring research skill, he should practice the techniques it suggests. He should examine the books, find the resources, make the telephone calls, write the letters, and so on.

There is no need to practice endlessly, like a Heifetz perfecting his skill on the violin. Gaining ability in research is more like learning to cook well. An excellent cook is not required to memorize five hundred recipes unless she wants to. But after a bit of practice she has learned how to use a dozen or more spices, when to sift the flour, how to control oven temperature, and where in her cookbooks to look up her favorite recipes.

It is the same with the techniques of research. You need enough practice to learn how to get quickly onto the trail of what you want to find out, and how to follow it to the end without being diverted. Practice in research work need not be lengthy or painful. But a certain amount of practice is essential to give you the "feel" of how to go about it, and the self-confidence to improvise new methods. Then absorbing new and more sophisticated technique becomes easier. Practice develops your ability to make the right moves from the start. Practice is what separates the pros from the amateurs.

The college freshman who learns and applies the Basic Techniques section of this book (pages 17–44) will have become a more skilled researcher than most college upperclassmen are today. The methods described here can be an aid to much better performance, and higher grades — particularly in writing papers for English, history and the social sciences. Unfortunately, college instructors often pay too little attention to showing lowerclassmen how to find information, in the campus library and elsewhere.

How to Read and Use This Book

This book is organized in three parts, the second of which (and by far the longest) is subdivided into three sections. These parts are:

You should first read through Part I (this part), because it explains how you can get the most from the book. Then read just as far in Part II as you can without becoming confused. In any case, you should read through Section A of Part II, on *Basic* Techniques of Research. As you read, decide on some practice exercises of your own, to test your grasp of Section A (basic techniques). Carry out these research projects as you go through Section A, or after reading the section, before starting on Section B (intermediate techniques).

I urge this because over the years I have found it useful to learn a variety of research techniques at the basic level, and how they can be used to complement one another, before taking up the more sophisticated techniques.

When you have a general grasp of Section A (basic techniques) then read on — and carry out some practice exercises — in Section B. After that try Section C. After reading and practice alternately, you can go back and carefully trace units on one subject (such as uses of indexes to periodicals) through all three sections — the basic, intermediate and advanced. Do this by referring to earlier related units on the subject marked *See First*, and then to later and usually more specialized or sophisticated material marked *Now See*.

The purpose of the Index (which is Part III) is to help you find passages and details under topics and proper names. Bear in mind that all index references are to the units in Part II, which is the main part of the book.

The research road is not limited to two dimensions like a route on a road map. It has many side-paths leading in many directions, like a tangle of scaffolding within a large building under construction. It would have been impossible to organize this book so that each subject would follow logically after another, enabling the reader to go through the book without ever needing to turn the pages back to look behind. For this reason, this text is made up of short units, each of which covers a subject that is sufficiently limited so that it can stand alone. You must determine for yourself which units are most important to you. Although some of the units within each section of Part II logically follow rather than precede others, the order within each section is to a great extent arbitrary.

The units are divided into three levels, or sections, labeled Basic, Intermediate and Advanced Techniques. Generally speaking, the Basic Techniques are most frequently used, the Intermediate next, and the Advanced would be employed last, or least often. When reading in the Intermediate and Advanced sections, you will probably find it wise to review the related units under a given subject in the Basic section, using the *See First* listing and the index, to make certain you have not overlooked a simpler or more general approach to that subject.

Mixing the Skills of Four Specialties

A first-class research worker needs techniques that combine the skills used by four kinds of professionals: the *reference librarian*, the *university scholar*, the *investigative reporter* and the *detective*. There is no reason for you to learn everything that these four specialists should know in order to do their jobs well. But the excellent researcher should learn certain essential skills used by each, and combine them so that they support one another. If you learn well, you come out with a broader and more generally useful range of abilities than any single one of these specialists commands.

It is by combining these abilities that you can become a skilled specialist in research.

The techniques described in this book are therefore a mix of source references, methods, tips and warnings that I have taken from the training of the librarian, the scholar, the reporter and the detective. I make no pretense that they are the ultimate methods, or the final word on the subject, because new techniques and resources are constantly emerging. What is new in this book, I believe, is the systematic mix of practical techniques taken from the scholarly, professional and business worlds and presented in a clear, logical form. I believe there is something new here for everyone, including the old pros.

A word now about the strong points, and the weaknesses, of the four types of professional whose special abilities contribute to this mix of research techniques.

1. *The Reference Librarian,* trained in a school of library science, often at a university, can be a masterful source of information on printed sources — especially reference books. He is usually as strong, and as broad in his knowledge, as the reference collection with which he works. This may mean an entire library, or only one part of a library. The most helpful general reference librarian I ever met was David Cole, who spent fifty years on the staff of the Library of Congress. Many times Mr. Cole revealed to me his amazingly detailed knowledge of the open-shelf collection of some 30,000 volumes in the alcoves around the main reading room, covering most subjects represented in that library. David Cole's breadth of knowledge was unusual. The average reference librarian, although an expert in his specialty, may know relatively little about sources outside his own collection. And he may be totally unaware of research techniques outside the reference library.

2. *The University Scholar* may be one of the world's most learned men within a limited field, and may be acquainted with every important book, manuscript collection, expert and other source bearing on his specialty. From him you can learn techniques that emphasize thoroughness. His research produces new information, or he brings to light facts that previously had been buried in written accounts lost in the darkness of libraries and archives. But too often the scholar in the humanities or social sciences works too slowly and within too narrow limits to suit the rest of us. We are operating in a world that makes fresh demands on us each day. We can admire the patience and thoroughness of the university scholar and yet remember the value of our time. This is not to express a lack of respect for the university scholar; it is only to say that our purposes are different. We can employ the best of his methods without living his life.

3. *The Investigative Reporter* is frequently an excellent all-around research worker, because the nature of his work has taught him to combine speed with thoroughness. His strength lies in his ability to interview the person or persons who witnessed an event, and to put an account of it in writing for the first time. A good reporter knows how to find his sources, how to ask the right questions, how to interpret responses, and where to find experts who can help him put today's event into the right context — and to do all this under pressure of a publication deadline. When a good reporter turns from daily newspaper reporting to writing a magazine article or a book, he studies background material from the library as the scholar does, though usually not so voluminously.

The principal difference in method between the news reporter and the scholar is that the reporter emphasizes completing his research so that he can produce the written account, whereas the scholar emphasizes the research process itself, with thoroughness as his goal, rather than publication for payment. For researchers, the art lies in combining the strong points of both. The reporter who has learned thoroughness of inquiry from the scholar can become an outstanding journalist, and Pulitzer prizes are won by such writers. The scholar who knows when to stop digging and to start shaping what he has found for presentation, and who is a skilled communicator, can become the author of best-selling books.

4. *The Detective* is frequently not far behind the investigative reporter in his all-around ability to find out what he wants to know — but he usually works within the limits of his world of law enforcement. His great asset as a researcher is his familiarity with human behavior patterns within his field. This enables him to cut through a confusion of details much more rapidly than the average person, and determine the handful of most probable places in which to search for answers. He is familiar with official documents, municipal archives, confidential indexes, credit ratings of individuals, and the like. His experience has taught him to reason out the most likely places in which to search for what he wants to know. More than anyone else, the fictional detective Sherlock Holmes taught the world the value of thinking a research problem through first — and then looking in the places that offer the greatest promise.

First Think Through Your Research·Plan

It was only after wasting considerable time in research for my own professional writing that I recognized the importance of thinking through a research project, and planning its general lines before digging in. The beginner often makes the mistake of rushing to the first possible source of information that occurs to him, when he should take a few minutes to consider several possible sources, then choose carefully the best order in which to follow them.

In research in history, biography and events of the recent past, particularly when you are looking for printed material, you can frequently get results if you play detective and ask yourself:

Who would know?
Who would care?
Who would care enough to have put it in print?

By following this procedure, the researcher might quickly come up with conclusions like these in specific cases:

What was the dollar value of the property loss in a recent big fire, or hurricane? Because insurance companies paid the property loss claims, they cared enough to compile their loss records. And because several companies must have been involved, the total loss figure is likely to have been compiled by the trade association of insurance companies — the American Insurance Association.

Another case: where should I look for biographical material on a distinguished American architect who died a few years ago? First, in the obituary pages of the daily newspaper in the city where he lived, because the local paper usually carries a more detailed obituary than papers in other cities. Second, in the pages of the periodical or journal of the special group of which he was a member — in this case the official organ of the American Institute of Architects.

The pages that follow abound in specifics on where to look for what kind of information. For the moment, my purpose is merely to stress the importance of stopping to THINK THROUGH YOUR PLAN OF RESEARCH. Five minutes may be enough, but pausing to think may save a fruitlessly wasted hour or day.

Four Ways to Find Out

Research is not all paperwork, or reading. There are four basic ways to find out what we want to know, and *Reading** is but one of them. The others, as I classify them, are:

Interviewing, or asking other people, both orally and in correspondence.

Observing for yourself.

Reasoning what must be the fact from what you have learned by other means.

In some research projects, using only one or two of these methods is sufficient to reach your desired end. But it is always worthwhile to remain alert to all four methods, in order to make sure that you have not overlooked a fruitful source or an important part of the story. Consider the four methods briefly:

1. *Reading.* Most of what people want to know has already been put on paper — somewhere, sometime. The difficulty for most of us lies in our not having the means, or the knowledge, to find the

---

*Here I classify the use of all audiovisual equipment (films, tapes, photographs, etc.) under *Reading*.

right books, articles, manuscripts and other written materials. We do not have *universal* subject indexes and in many parts of the country it is difficult to obtain some written materials about which we know. A large part of this book is devoted to showing how to search for written materials and to get your hands on them.

2. *Interviewing the Expert or Source-Person.* When facts we want have not been put in writing, at least not to our knowledge, we can try to find the people who know and ask them. (Example: the survivors of a disaster of years ago which has not been fully documented; or intimates of a political figure, now dead, who can discuss the behind-the-scenes actions of their late friend or relative.) The interviewer's written account of what such source-people tell him then may become the first document on the subject.

Interviewing and reading are closely connected, and they complement each other. Reading can lead the researcher to the source-person who can fill in gaps in the written record. And those we interview can often point us toward written sources that we have not yet used. (Example: biographers who track down surviving relatives or friends of their subject often discover valuable documents that have long lain untouched and unknown in attic and basement.)

3. *Observing for Ourselves.* When what we want to know has not been put satisfactorily in writing, and when we cannot find anyone who can tell us, we must sometimes observe for ourselves, using our own eyes and ears. This is the method of research basic to the natural sciences and to exploration, such as the space flights of the astronauts, or Robert E. Peary's trek by dog sledge over the Arctic ice to the North Pole, or Columbus' voyages across the Atlantic Ocean. In research for books of history, biography and even for fiction, the writer often finds it useful to immerse himself in his locale in order to gather information of an atmospheric nature — how things look, feel, sound and smell. Such direct observation is interwoven with reading and interviewing.

4. *Reasoning from What We Have Learned.* Concluding what must have happened, or what must be the case now, from facts we have learned by other means is the most elusive and dangerous method of fact-finding. It is heavily employed by vertebrate paleontologists, archaeologists and geologists, whose science rests on reasoned conclusions from evidence in the earth. It is the method most *misused* by historians and biographers. (Example: the many so-called "lives" of William Shakespeare, the playwright-poet,

rest shakily on the skimpiest of documentation, and are pasted together with presumptive terms such as "probably," "can be assumed to," "perhaps," "is supposed to," and the like.)

Reasoning from the known to the unknown in research is best used as a method that leads to new documents and sources, and therefore to finding more than standard bibliographies and other sources have provided. It is a method that should be used from the beginning in drawing up a research plan, in order that the *most likely* sources are covered before those that are merely *possible* sources.

Five Classes of Written Materials

Too much research time is wasted in hunting for the written materials we need, when it might be spent productively in using them. Therefore, an important element in research skill lies in getting your hands on the right material fast.

I divide reading matter into five general classes because the methods for locating materials in each differ, and so are best explained separately. These classes are:

1. Published books

2. Magazines and journals (learned society periodicals)

3. Newspapers

4. Special *duplicated* documents that are *not published* (that is, not *generally* and freely circulated) and not copyrighted. Examples: reports of organizations intended for internal or restricted use; rosters of organization members; calendars of organization activities; newsletters of small organizations, etc.

5. Manuscripts (or "papers"), meaning *unpublished and unduplicated* documents, such as letters, notes and diaries. These are generally handwritten or typewritten. Most historians and librarians use the terms *manuscripts* and *papers* interchangeably.

Strictly for convenience in organizing this book I have classed various specialized written sources under the five headings above. Example: *newsletters* fall under the *magazines* heading. The reader can locate them in the Index.

Be Realistic About Purpose, Time and Cost

The right way to go about a research project can vary according to the time, money and manpower available, and the purpose of your search. To write a weekly paper for an undergraduate college course, a student can afford only so much time. For this purpose it does not make sense to travel to a distant city in order to consult books in a major library for a half day. But for a doctoral dissertation a serious graduate student will cross the country to study the rare books and the manuscripts which the task requires. For a definitive book or magazine article, a skilled and conscientious writer will take every bit of pains required to gather fresh data. A hack writer, on the other hand, will crank out books and articles simply by reading and reorganizing what more conscientious researchers have written from original sources. This is the case because the hack writing market does not pay enough to permit more thorough and careful work.

The desired end result, or purpose, should bear some sensible relation to the time and money spent in research. A busy professional in the thirty-thousand-dollar-a-year class should spend twenty dollars without hesitation for Xerox copies that will save him a day's work, whereas a student of age twenty-one might well choose to save the money. Or if a few dollars' worth of long distance telephone calls will speed up a committee chairman's work by several days, the money is well spent.

Unless the purpose of a research project is to exhaust every conceivable resource in a given search, you can set your own commonsense limits. In presenting the more sophisticated research techniques contained in the Advanced Techniques section (pages 89-116) I trust that users of this book will remember that the name of the game is not *Search*, but *Find Out*. If the last 10 percent of your planned research time has brought excellent results, you are doubtless on a productive new track and should extend the project. But if the last 25 percent of your scheduled time has brought greatly diminished results, this fact is a signal to wind up your research. It all depends, however, on your having established a productive plan for you research project at the outset.

II. Techniques of Research

A. BASIC TECHNIQUES

Finding the Right Library

"Just go to the library and look it up." Easily said, but not always so easily done. "The library" may be no help if the one to which you go does not have what you need, or if you cannot find in it what you need.

Most people live within reach of a number of libraries — more than they know — and some of these libraries can serve their needs much better than others. It is useful to learn what each of the following types of library in your area has to offer: (1) the **public** library system (city, county or state libraries); (2) the **college and university** libraries; (3) **school** libraries; and (4) the **special** libraries, so called because they are devoted to collections of limited subjects, and are usually run by private organizations such as historical societies, corporations, social agencies, museums. Most people know little or nothing about the many thousands of special libraries, and special subject collections within general libraries, literally hundreds of which may be right in their own metropolitan area.

A first step in surveying the local library resources is to ask an experienced professional librarian (NOT just anyone behind the checkout desk). The head librarian is usually a member of the American Library Association and therefore has contact with his/ her professional colleagues in the same city.

A second step is to consult the *American Library Directory* (published by R. R. Bowker Co.). This massive reference work can usually be found in the librarian's office, if it is not at the reference desk. It lists more than 30,000 libraries in the United States, and 3,000 in Canada. Listings are arranged geographically by state and city. Each entry has enough detail to tell you whether that particular library is worth visiting or telephoning with your query.

§S FEDERAL DEPOSIT INSURANCE CORP, Chicago Region Library,* Sears Tower, 233 S Wacker Dr, Suite 6116, 60606. Tel 353-0700

S FEDERAL RESERVE BANK OF CHICAGO LIBRARY, 230 S LaSalle St, 60604. Tel 322-5828. Founded 1922. *Librn* Jo Ann Aufdenkamp. Staff 9 (prof 5, nonprof 4) Bk titles 12,000; Per sub 600, vols bd 3000. VF 250
Subject interests: Agr econ, bus conditions, cent banking, monetary policy, statistics
Partic in Ill Regional Libr Coun; Chicago Libr Syst

§S FEDERAL TRADE COMMISSION, Chicago Regional Office Library,* 55 E Monroe St, 60603. Tel 353-4423

R FELICIAN COLLEGE LIBRARY, 3800 W Peterson Ave, 60659. Tel 539-2328. Founded 1953. Enr 111; Fac 11. *Dir* Sr Mary M Chrysantha Rudnik; *Asst Dir* Sr Mary M Julianne Chudy. Staff 4 (prof 2, cler 2)
1974-75 Inc $10,735 (incl fed $4235). Exp $5000, Bks $2910, Per $1766, AV $324 Bk titles 28,956, vols 38,061; Per sub 159, vols bd 5045, micro 123. Micro Hldgs: Fiche 12, Reels 126. AV: Rec, A-Tapes, Flm, Fs, Slides, Ov tr, Maps, Cht, Art repro. VF 20
Special subjects: Art-archit, hist, lit, minority studies, relig, soc & behav sci, ethnic studies
Mem of Chicago Pub Libr
Bk purchasing ctr: Midwest Libr Serv
Partic in Ill Libr Network & Ohio Col Libr Ctr

§S FIBRA-SONICS, INC LIBRARY,* 4626 N Lamon Ave, 60630. Tel 286-7377. *Librn* Marge McCall

S FIELD ENTERPRISES EDUCATIONAL CORP, Research Library, Merchandise Mart Plaza, 60654. Tel 341-8777. Founded 1920. Servs ed, art & res depts of Corp *Head Librn* Vera G Busselle. Staff 5 (prof 3, nonprof 2)
Bk titles 13,400, vols 20,000; Per sub 600, vols bd 10 (titles), micro 7 (titles). Micro Hldgs: Reels 647. AV: Maps. VF 300
Partic in Ill Regional Libr Coun

S FIELD MUSEUM OF NATURAL HISTORY LIBRARY, Roosevelt Rd & Lake Shore Dr, 60605. Tel 922-9410, Ext 282. Founded 1893. *Librn* W Peyton Fawcett. Staff 9 (prof 5, nonprof 4)
1975 Exp $55,000, Bks $20,000, Per $26,000, Bd $9000; Sal $92,500 (prof $61,600, nonprof $30,900) Bk titles 70,000, vols 85,000; Per sub 2500, vols bd 100,000, micro 100. Micro Hldgs: 100. AV: Rec, Maps
Subject interests: Anthropology, archeology, botany, Far Eastern studies, geol, paleontology, zoology, museology
Special collections: Ornithology (Edward E Ayer Ornithology Library); Herpetology (Karl P Schmidt Herpetology Library), bks & reprints

S FIRST NATIONAL BANK OF CHICAGO LIBRARY, One First National Plaza, 60670. Tel 732-3590. Founded 1931. Pvt libr for staff & to mems of Ill Regional Libr Coun; ILL. *Librn* Martha Whaley. Staff 10 (prof 4, nonprof 6)
Bk titles 12,000; Per sub 300, vols bd 30, micro 20. VF 150
Partic in Ill Libr & Info Network; Ill Regional Libr Coun

S FOLLETT PUBLISHING CO, Editorial Library,* 1010 W Washington Blvd, 60607. Tel 666-5855
Bk vols 4000 (incl bd per)

S HARRIS TRUST & SAVINGS B, St, 60690. Tel 461-2121. *Librn* M1 Bk vols 4500

§S HEALTH & HOSPITALS GOVER LIBRARY,* 1900 W Polk St, 6061? Partic in MEDLINE

§S HEIDRICK & STRUGGLES INC, 1
_____ ?argar

R MED ?12. Tel

r Rosc uly. *Li* s bd 10?

)RMATI 1974. *L.* Per $4? ab 66. ?)

?

MEDIC? zabeth C ?nsorti

N, MUI ?0670. T

The **American Library Directory** is the definitive directory used by professional librarians in the United States and Canada. Listings are arranged geographically by state and city.

S HOUSEHOLD FINANCE CORP I Tel 944-7174. *Librn* Nancy G Wa Bk vols 8000

S DANIEL D HOWARD ASSOC 60601. Tel 372-7041. Subject interests: Bus

S ILLINOIS BELL TELEPHONE 727-2668. Founded 1910. Staff onl? nonprof 3)
Ann Exp $7000, Bks $4000, Per $ nonprof $37,000)
Bk titles 18,000, vols 20,000; Per vc Subject interests: Business mgt, tech, Special collections: History of Illino? Library)
Partic in Chicago Pub Libr ILL Netw

S ILLINOIS BUREAU OF EMPLO? 910 S Michigan, 60606. Tel 793-40? Bk vols 1500

M ILLINOIS CENTRAL HOSPIT? Ave, 60637. Tel 643-9200

HINDI LANGUAGE AND LITERATURE
Library of Congress Orientalia Division
Washington, D C 20540
Cat Mss Maps Pix Slides Microforms
Notes Southern Asian Almost 98,000 vols
Literature of the area from Pakistan to the
Philippines, espec Bengali, Marathi, Hindi, Urdu,
Nepali, Indonesian, Vietnamese, Thai, Burmese
University of Michigan, Graduate Library Om P
Sharma, South Asian Bibliographer Ann Arbor,
Mich 48104
Cat Maps Slides Microforms
Notes The major emphasis is on social sciences
and humanities Besides materials in classical
languages South Asian vernaculars being
retained are Hindi, Bengali, Urdu, Marathi and
Tamil
New York Public Library, Oriental Division John L
Mish, Chief Fifth Ave & 42 St , New York, N.Y.
10018
Cat Mss Microforms
Notes Published catalog of holdings.
University of Pennsylvania, Van Pelt Library 34 and
Walnut Sts , Philadelphia, Pa. 19104
Vols 35,000 Cat
Notes Incl South Asia social sciences, history,
politics, economics and anthropology. Extensive
holdings in vernacular languages, especially
Hindi, Tamil and Sanskrit

HINDUISM
Cleveland Public Library Alice N. Loranth, Head,
John G White Dept 325 Superior Ave ,
Cleveland Ohio 44114
Vols 7000 Cat Mss Pix
Notes Emphasis is on religious texts in their
original languages and Western translations
Treatises on religious beliefs and practices are
also incl Strong holdings in Buddhism, Egyptian
religion, Hinduism, Judaica, Lamaistic texts,
Mohammedanism, Sikhism and Zoroastrianism
Works on primitive religion cover aspects of
animism, totemism, fetishism, etc A strong
collection on classical religious beliefs and
mythology serves as comparative material.
Special emphasis on Mohammedanism in China
University of Pennsylvania, Van Pelt Library 34 and
Walnut Sts , Philadelphia, Pa. 19104
Cat Mss
Notes Almost 3000 mss, from the 15th to the
19th centuries, mostly on philosophy, religion
and grammar

HINE, LEWIS W.
New York Public Library Gunther E. Pohl, Chief,

Vols (159,450)
Notes Books, papers, mss, etc, by and about

HISPANIA, ROMAN VISIGOTHIC see
Roman: Visigothic Hispania

HISPANIC CIVILIZATION see Civilization, Hispanic

HISPANO AMERICAN WAR, 1898 see U S —
History—War of 1898

HISTOLO_
Carnegi_
Head
Forbe
Vols
Budg_
Notes
becau_
with f
the C_
coope_
provis_
some
There
specia_

> Organized
> by subject,
> **Subject Collections**
> is a guide to special
> libraries and
> special collections
> within general
> libraries. (Lee Ash).

HISTOPLASMOSIS
Parker-Davis Memorial Library William L Jellison,
Dir 504 S Third St , Hamilton, Mont. 59840
Vols 500 Uncat Mss
Notes Zoonoses and related diseases Incl
Mss, notes, correspondence of Dr R R Parker,
Dr Gordon E Davis, Dr Edward Francis

HISTORIC AMERICAN BUILDINGS SURVEY
Library of Congress, Prints and Photographs
Division Washington, D.C. 20540
Cat Pix

HISTORICAL CRITICISM see Historiography

HISTORICAL FICTION
University of Pittsburgh Libraries, Special
Collections Department, Hervey Allen Collection
Charles E Aston, Jr , Coordinator 363 Hillman
Library, Pittsburgh, Pa. 15260
Vols (2000) Cat Mss Maps Pix
Correspondence
Budget ($1000)
Notes Emphasis on American historical fiction

HISTORICAL GEOGRAPHY see Geography,
Historical

As a third step, you can consult a companion to the *American
Library Directory* (mentioned above) entitled: *Subject Collections*, edited by Lee Ash (published by R. R. Bowker Co., 5th
edition, 1978). This reference book (which I call *Lee Ash* for convenience) is organized by subject, and within the subject categories
entries are arranged alphabetically in geographic order. Whereas
the *American Library Directory* lists entire libraries, *Lee Ash* lists

not only special libraries devoted to one subject, but also special collections of books within general libraries. There may, for instance, be several special collections (e.g., Indian art, cooking, baseball, etc.) within one general library. *Lee Ash* lists each collection under the subject heading, whereas the *American Library Directory* lists them under the library's name.

One other aid to finding special libraries is the *Directory of Special Libraries and Information Centers*, published by Gale Research Co. This book has nearly 14,000 entries, which serve as a useful cross-check on those in the two other directories mentioned above. Volume I is organized alphabetically, and is indexed by subject. There is a geographical breakdown in Volume II, by name of state, city and town, but not by metropolitan area. For this reason is requires considerable hunting in important subjects like art, or engineering, to find all the entries describing special libraries in a big city or within a convenient distance of any major city.

In choosing which library to use, remember that the total size of the library is less important to you than the strength of its collection in the subject field in which you are interested. Usually the special library will have a more thorough collection of materials (books, periodicals, manuscripts, illustrations and maps) in its particular field than will any but the greatest general library. In addition to the depth of its collections, the special library offers other advantages to the researcher. First, its experienced staff members will usually have more detailed knowledge of the materials under their care than one can expect from the reference librarians in a general library who are not specialists. Second, the special library staff is likely to have more time to serve the needs of a reader because they have much less reader traffic to deal with. Third, the special library is likely to be more quiet, and may offer easier access to duplicating equipment or a typing room.

Some who would like to use a private special library (such as a corporate or law firm library) are afraid that they would not be permitted to use it because, in principle, it is not open to the public. In a very few cases this may be so. But usually the librarian in charge of a private special library will extend the courtesy of its use to an outsider who approaches her giving evidence of having a serious intent. The writer has used many private collections, offering no special credentials, and has never been turned away at the door.

★7230★
PABST BREWING COMPANY - P-L BIOCHEMICALS, INC. - RESEARCH LIBRARY (Food-Bev)
1037 W. McKinley Ave.   Phone: (414) 271-0230
Milwaukee, WI 53205   Marie Fendry, Res.Libn.
Founded: 1944. Staff: 1. Subjects: Microbiology, biochemistry, chemistry. Holdings: 1932 books; 1450 bound periodical volumes; 3198 pamphlets. Subscriptions: 75 journals and other serials. Services: Library not open to public

★7231★
PACE COMPANIES - LIBRARY (Sci-Tech: Env-Cons)
Box 53495   Phone: (713) (
Houston, TX 77052   Joyce R. Bax
Founded: 1953. Staff: Prof 2. Subjects: Petroleum refining tec
petrochemical plant design; natural gas processing; envir(
engineering; energy analysis and forecasting, business statistics.
6000 books; 600 bound periodical volumes; 2000 company repor
Bureau of Mines reports; 1200 manuscripts and patents; 340,000 tech
clippings; 2000 microforms. Subscriptions: 225 journals and othe
Services: Interlibrary loans; copying; library open to public by app
Staff: Laura P. Pilgram, Asst.Libn.

★7232★
PACE UNIVERSITY - LIBRARY (Bus-Fin)
Pace Plaza   Phone: (212) 285-3551
New York, NY 10038   Henry Birnbaum, Dir. Of Libs.
Staff: Prof 11; Other 20. Subjects: Liberal arts and sciences, accounting, finance, management, marketing, real estate, taxation. Holdings: 207,000 books and bound periodical volumes; corporation annual reports for 2500 companies; 17,000 pamphlets; 15,500 reels of microfilm. Subscriptions: 1200 journals and other serials; 6 newspapers. Services: Interlibrary loans; copying; library open to public for reference use only. Automated Operations: Microreproduction. Staff: Janice Axton, Ref.Libn.; Bruce J. Bergman, Asst.Dir. Of Libs.; Joseph Hores, Per.Libn.; Nina Moinester, Educ.Libn.; Purificacion Quebengco, Acq.Libn.; Rachelle Rosenberg, Cat.; Mrs. Khung-Sook Koh, Cat.; Thomas Snyder, Ref.Libn.; Anne Takacs, Circ.Libn.; Daisy Wong, Hd.Cat.

★7233★
PACE UNIVERSITY, WESTCHESTER - LIBRARY (Bus-Fin)
861 Bedford Rd.   Phone: (914) 769-3200
Pleasantville, NY 10570   Mary Vie Cramblitt, Libn
Founded: 1963. Staff: Prof·6; Other 4. Subjects: Business administration, period histories, accounting, nursing, 19th century English literature, computer science. Holdings: 108,384 books and bound periodical volumes; 3001 pamphlets; 987 corporation reports; 293 college bulletins; 5222 reels of microfilm. Subscriptions: 656 journals and other serials. Services: Interlibrary loans; copying; library open to public for reference use only. Automated Operations: Microreproduction. Networks/Consortia: Member of Westchester Library System. Staff: Louise Wagner, Acq./Per.Libn.; Eva Louise Reiman, Rd.Serv.Libn.; Kevin A. Ryan, Tech.Serv.Libn.

★7234★
PACIFIC AND ASIAN AFFAIRS COUNCIL - PACIFIC HOUSE LIBRARY (Area-Ethnic)
2004 University Ave.   Phone: (808) 941-5355
Honolulu, HI 96816
Founded: 1925. Staff: Prof 4; Other 2. Subjects: Info.

★7236★
PACIFIC CHRISTIAN COLL
2500 E. Nutwood Ave.
Fullerton, CA 92631
Founded: 1929. Staff: Prof
church history, Bible, mi
                               ,50 t
                               thes
                               0 re
                               als,
                               :s,
                               1: [
                               sca

The **Directory**
of Special Libraries
and Information
Centers (Gale)
offers detailed
information on
each entry in
Volume I.
Geographic breakdown is in
Volume II.

                               NG
                               50·

                               e
                               ne
                               es:

PACIFIC COLLEGE - MENN
See: Mennonite Brethren E

★7238★
PACIFIC GAS AND ELECT
77 Beale St.
San Francisco, CA 9410(
Founded: 1906. Staff: Pr
Services: Library not ope

★7239★
PACIFIC GAS AND ELECT
77 Beale St.
San Francisco, CA 94106
Staff: Prof 2; Other 2. Sut
business, science. Spec
and bound periodical v
other serials. Services:
Library Bulletin, month

★7240★
PACIFIC HOSPITAL OF LO(
2776 Pacific Ave.
Long Beach, CA 90801
Staff: Prof 1; Other 2.
administration, acupunctur
including charts of acupu
titles. Holdings: 5000 boo
pamphlets and reprints. S
Interlibrary loans; copyin
when user is sponsored b
staff and er

Finding Special Libraries in Your City

See First:
Finding the Right Library (p 17)

One of the most valuable research aids that you can acquire is a list or directory of the special libraries in your own metropolitan area — one you can keep on your own desk. This is especially true of large cities like New York and Washington, where the special library resources are so great. Unless you have copies of the *American Library Directory* or *Lee Ash* or the Gale *Directory* at hand, you can save time by consulting a local directory of special libraries at will, within reach of your own telephone and typewriter.

Many professional librarians in special libraries are members of the Special Libraries Association (SLA). In a number of cities the SLA members have formed chapters and have published lists or directories of their members (both librarians and libraries). An especially useful example is the *Special Libraries Directory of Greater New York* (published by SLA, New York Chapter). This paperbound directory gives details on more than 1,200 special libraries in New York City and environs. It is carefully indexed by subject matter specialties and by names of libraries and librarians.

The simple way to find out whether there is such a directory or list in your own city is to ask a member of the SLA — whom you can find in a local library listed in *Lee Ash* or the Gale *Directory*. If there is such a local list, it may be found at the reference desk of a general library. It is usually kept out of sight, or in the librarian's office, for the use of the staff and not for readers. But if you ask, you can get it.

CAUTION: Do not automatically accept the word of a library assistant that there is no such list in your city, because frequently assistants do not know. Check with the head librarian, or an SLA member, to be sure. If there is such a directory, even if it is only a mimeographed list, it pays to obtain a copy and examine it.

Dealing with Librarians

The professional librarian is a graduate of a school of library science and has been through a rigorous discipline leading to the master's degree. In the course of the training she has been exposed to a wide range of reference materials, and should be able to guide readers to them.

It is well worth the trouble for the serious research worker to cultivate the acquaintance of librarians in a position to help. Librarians serve so many people who never even say "thank you"

BEHAVIORAL SCIENCES

AMERICAN SOCIETY FOR PSYCHICAL RESEARCH LIBRARY, 5 West 73rd St, New York, NY (10023). ●212-799-5050. Founded 1905.

MAJOR SUBJECTS Psychical research (parapsychology), spiritualism, religion, philosophy, psychology. SPECIAL COLLECTIONS Shaker materials, unpublished card index to Society's Journal & Proceedings. Rhea A. White*, Director of Information. Staff: 1. Mon-Fri 10-5.

Vols 8,000 not incl bd per. PT 60. Micro reels 26. VFD 42. For members, scholars, students. I P

ANALYTICAL PSYCHOLOGY CLUB OF NEW YORK INC, KRISTINE MANN LIBRARY, 28 East 39th St, New York, NY (10016). ●212-697-7877 Founded 1945.

MAJOR SUBJECTS Psychology of C.G. Jung (analytical psychology, mythology, comparative religion, alchemy, symbolism, anthropology). SPECIAL COLLECTIONS Complete publications of Jung & other writers in the field, Bollingen series Jung Press Archive (in preparation). Doris B. Albrecht, Librarian. Staff: (1 prof). Mon 1:15-8:45, Tues-Fri 10:15-5:45.

Vols 5,000 incl bd per. PT 7. VFD 27. For public, members, scholars & students.

BETH ISRAEL MEDICAL CENTER, MEDICAL LIBRARY, BERNSTEIN INSTITUTE BRANCH, Morris J. Bernstein Institute, 307 Second Ave, New York, NY (10003). ●212-677-2300, Ext 256. Founded 1969.

MAJOR SUBJECTS Psychiatry, psychology, social work, drug addiction & alcoholism. Arlene L. Freedman*, Director of Medical Libraries, 673-3000, Ext 4250. Dagmar S. Scott, Reference. Staff: 1. Mon-Fri 9-5.

Vols 3,000 incl bd per. PT 130. VFD 10. For staff, others by appt. I Dagmar S. Scott, Ext 256. P

BRONX PSYCHIATRIC CENTER, THE KAY RICHEY LIBRARY, 1500 Waters Pl, Bronx, NY (10461). ●212-931-0600, Ext 2348 or 2572.

MAJOR SUBJECTS Psychiatry, psychology, social work. Kathryn S. Connolly, Acting Librarian. Staff: 1. Mon-Fri 8-4.

Vols 3,560 not incl bd per. PT 485. Micro reels 10. MRP. VFD 5. For staff only. I P

MAJOR SUBJECTS Psychiatr psychology, medicine, rehabili' work. Mrs Emily R. Lehrman Librarian, Ext 273. Staff: 2 (1 9-4.

Vols 2,000 not incl bd per. P1 For staff. I P

128 **CENTER OF ALCOHOL STUI LIBRARY,** Rutgers University, Documentation/Publication Divi Campus, New Brunswick, NJ (0: 1957. /
grist &
n Spec
her.

ihol &
ddicti
medi
iciolo
etc.
d Ab
umul
ige-n
ng C,
ect t
liter
Lib

Beck, Lorraine Lowry, Joan Zimmermann, Mrs Pei Lan Staff: 15 (9 prof). Mon-Fri

Vols 6,800 incl bd per. . PT 550 (dissertations). MRP. VF boxes). For faculty, students, members & other librarians. I

129 **CENTRAL ISLIP PSYCHIAT HEALTH SCIENCE LIBRAR** Ave Rehabilitation Bldg 2nd f NY (11722). ●516-234-6262 E

MAJOR SUBJECTS Psychiat psychology, psychoanalysis, n types); internal medicine & al Sandra Meyer, Librarian. Stat M-F 8-4:30.

Vols 3,427 not incl bd per. PT VFD 15. for staff, students, SL and other libns. I Helen Conne other libraries. P Helen Conne'

130 **CENTRAL ISLIP STATE HO HEALTH SCIENCE LIBRAR** Rehabilitation Bldg, Central I (11722). ●516-234-6262, Ext : MAJOR SUBJECTS psychiat psychology, psychoanalysis, ni

that they welcome a library user who speaks to them by name and shows appreciation for their knowledge and help. For a person with whom she has a friendly relationship, a librarian will often look up material in response to a telephone query — saving the researcher a trip. And when the librarian takes a personal interest in the researcher's project, she may over a period of time bring to his attention a number of source materials that he has overlooked. In this way, the librarian-friend can be a highly useful and skilled research ally.

Take the time to search out a really first-class reference librarian to whom you can turn confidently for help. Unfortunately, libraries sometimes employ people who will say, "We don't have it," when they really do not know, or who will dismiss your research queries with only minimum effort to help. Mark such klunks and shun them. The librarian to seek out is the one who takes every request for help as a challenge to see if she and her library's resources can meet your research needs.

The Best Guide to Reference Books

Of all the lists of reference books available, I find the most useful and best edited is *Reference Books: A Brief Guide* (pub. by Enoch Pratt Free Library, 400 Cathedral Street, Baltimore, Md. 21201). This 180-page papeback costs $2.50. If you cannot find it locally in bookstores that service a school of library science, you can order it by mail from the Enoch Pratt Free Library. New editions appear at intervals of four or five years.

By keeping this little book at hand and becoming familiar with it, the student and researcher can save time by first determining which reference books appear most useful for his inquiry, then telephoning to find which of them are available at local libraries. Because so many reference books are so well described in this source booklet (which I term, for convenience, *Enoch Pratt*) I strongly urge readers to obtain their own copy. An alternative is to use a library copy, and that is preferable to not using it at all. (For convenience in searching for it in a card catalogue, note that it was compiled by Marion V. Bell and Eleanor A. Swidan, whose names are printed on author cards.)

It would be wasteful to duplicate in these pages the descriptions of many reference books, and tips on how to use them, carried in *Enoch Pratt*. It is much better to have your own copy — and use it.

Now See:
The Librarian's Guide to Reference Books (p. 93)

Finding Reference Books in Libraries

See First:
The Best Guide to Reference Books (p. 24)
Dealing with Librarians (p. 22)

It is well worth the time to ask a librarian (or more than one) whether there is a standard reference book that covers the field in which you are seeking information. At the start, random searching through the open reference shelves wastes more time than it is worth. You can consult the library card catalog to find out whether the library has a certain book whose title you know, but usually the librarians are familiar with their most frequently used reference books and can tell you where they are shelved. Because some of these books have considerable commercial value, they are frequently kept behind the circulation desk to be handed out only on request.

After consulting *Enoch Pratt* (p. 24) or another similar guide to reference books, it is most effective to start by asking a librarian for help in general terms. Go to the specific, or detailed, later. The reason for this is that a typical librarian is more likely to know the category in which a book is classified than to know the details it contains. Therefore, it would usually be more productive to start by asking for a standard reference book on hotels, rather than to ask where you can find how big the Mayflower Hotel in Washington is. Once she has shown you the annual *Hotel Red Book*, published by the American Hotel Association, you can find your own answer — or ask for further help.

I have had good results by approaching librarians with a query phrased something like this:

"What standard reference books do you have in the field of *(general)*? What I am trying to find out is *(specific)*." An especially good librarian may suggest more than one title, all of them useful. She may go further and bring in a book that pinpoints the object of a reader's research. But this is a matter of luck — rarely encountered in a general library, though much more often in a special library. As you become more experienced in research, you become familiar with the specific reference books and other sources that you have found useful and can go directly to them.

The New York Times Index

The New York Times Index, bound in annual volumes, contains brief abstracts of the contents of that newspaper, arranged chronologically under subject headings, with date, page and column references. It is the best quick source of information on events of the past several decades because: (1) it is so widely distributed in

PROVIDENCE College
  7 students are killed and 16 others injured when fire envelopes women's dormitory; names of victims noted; fire, considered city's worst since 1800's, is termed accidental; Gov J Joseph Garrahy comments; illus (M), D 14,22:4; illus of student waiting for rescue by firemen, D 14,1:1; James Bennett, pres of Local 799 of Fire Fighters Union, cites lack of sufficient manpower and new equipment as factor in deaths; says death of fire lieut might have been avoided if city had 4 firefighters, instead of 3, on each fire truck (S), D 15,18:5; funeral mass is held for Donna B Galligan; 18 priests are among mourners; funeral services also held for victims Kathryn Andresakes and Deborah Smith; illus (M), D 17,53:4; students Sallyann Garvey and Dorothy A Widman die of burns, bringing death total to 9 (S), D 28,IV,16:6
PROVIDENCE Gas Co. See also Gas—US, Mr 1
PROVIDENCE Journal-Bulletin (RI). See also News—US—Awards, Ap 21
PROVIDENT National Bank of Philadelphia. See also Mitchell Energy & Development Corp, My 27
PROVIDENT National Corp. See also div and subsidiary names, eg, Maguire, John P, & Co
PROVIDENT Savings Bank (Jersey City, NJ). See also First National Bank (Dunellen, NJ), Ag 26
PROVINCETOWN Playhouse (Mass)
  2 youths are arrested in connection with fire that damaged Provincetown Playhouse (S), Mr 28,57:6
PROVITERA, Henry. See also Counterfeiting, F 16
PROVITERA, John H. See also Counterfeiting, F 16
PROXMIRE, Elsie Stillman
  Sen William Proxmire and Mrs Miles McMillin announce engagement of daughter, Elsie Stillman Proxmire, to Dr Alan Robert Zwerner, son of David and Mrs Zwerner; Elsie's por (S), Ja 16,50:3
PROXMIRE, William (Sen). See also
Airplanes—US—Mil Aircraft, N 4
Armament etc, O 24
Atomic Energy—Atomic Weapons, F 8
Banks—US, Ja 2, Je 30, Ag 22, S 4,17,27, D 19
Chauffeurs and Drivers, My 6
Communications Satellites, Ja 26
Credit (Genl)—US, N 10,12, D 30
Credit (Genl)—US—Consumer Credit, N 9
Econ Conditions (Genl), D 7
Elections (US)—Finances, Ja 16, My 4, Ja 16
Energy and Power, Je 14, O 26
Firemen—NYC, D 29
Freedom, Mr 26
Gas—US—Pipelines, Ag 16
Govt Bonds, D 2
Housing—Indiana—Discrimination, Jl 16
Housing—NYC—Rents and Renting, D 8
Housing—NYS, Je 1
Housing—US, Ja 11, Je 1, N 10
Hutchinson, Ronald R, Ja 7, My 2
Intl Rel—Communist-Western, Ja 8,31, F 1
Iran, Jl 12
Lance, Thomas Bertram (Dir), Ag 20,22,29, S 4,17,28
Middle East—Israeli-Arab Conflict, F 22, O 24
Missiles, D 27
NYC—Finances—Expense Budget, Ja 14,24,25, My 18, A 29, S 23,24, D 6,8,11,16,17,28,29
  Employees, D 29

PRUTETZEL, Maria. See also Prinze, Freddie, Jl 20
PRUYN, Kenyon W. See also Murders—NYS, Je 29
PRYCE-Jones, David. See also France—Pol, D 11
PRYOR, David H (Gov). See also Arkansas—Election N 29, D 4,11. US—Econ Conditions—Southern State Ap 2
PRYOR, Donald J (Msgr). See also Educ—NYS—Sec Schools, D 7
PRYOR, Karen. See also Fish—Fishing, Commercial,
PRYOR, Rich
  Pictures—R(
  Pictures—R(
  Pictures—R(
  Programs. P
  Special Shov
    Hospitalize
  (S), N 11,II,
PSA Peugeot
  Rcpts '76 (
  of $7.1-milli(
PSITTACOSIS
PSORIASIS
  NY Atty (
  Queens psori
  operations ar
  public; says t
  FDA; center
PSUITY, Norn
  Gateway Na
PSYCHIATRIC
US. Ap 5, S

> Annual index to
> **The New York Times**
> lists all articles
> printed in the year
> by subject, with
> many cross-references,
> and gives date of issue,
> page and column.
> Section of Sunday
> issues is in Roman
> numerals.

PSYCHIATRI
S 25. USSR—Pol, Ag 22,23,31, S 1,2,4,9,18, O 29
  Meets, Ag 22,23:6; Ag 31,8:4; meets (S), S 1,8:2; S rev of Gen Assembly resolution (S), S 4,IV,14:3
PSYCHIATRISTS, Royal College of (GB). See also US Pol, S 2
PSYCHIATRY, Institute of (London, Eng). See also Alcoholism, S 25. Autism, Ap 24

PSYCHIATRY and Psychiatrists. Use Mental Health a Disorders
PSYCHIC Phenomena
  Several hundred people attend 'psychic fair' held at Foundation Faith of the Millennium, NYC (M), Ja 1
  Prof George Steiner article asserts growing beliefs paranormal and psychic phenomena could lead to str renaissance of theological thought and argument; dra (M), D 9,27:2
  R Baker article on various kinds of ghosts he has encountered (M), D 24,19:1; Ir on Dec 9 article, D 2

PSYCHOANALYTIC Societies, International Federation
See also Psychology, Ag 21

PSYCHOLOGICAL Assn, American. See also Families, S 2. Murders—NYC, Ag 27. Psychology, D 3. Weig Ag 29
  Conv session, San Francisco (S), S 2,12:1
PSYCHOLOGICAL Assn, California. See also Mental Health—US, Ap 5
PSYCHOLOGICAL Warfare. See Propaganda, War par

American libraries; (2) the *Times*'s coverage of events has been so extensive since it became a great newspaper early in the twentieth century; and (3) the indexing is so thorough.

For the current year *The New York Times Index* is cumulated and issued semimonthly, and reaches subscribing libraries in paper cover. These are usually kept in a box near the latest bound volume. The *Index* for past years since 1930 is bound in annual volumes, deep maroon in color, which are distributed in late spring of the new year. For the 1913–30 period, the *Index* in most libraries is in quarterly volumes, although some have it in semiannual volumes. Between 1851 (the starting year) and 1912, each volume contains two or more years. The researcher should be alert to these differences in format when looking for an indexed item some years back.

Primary value of using *The New York Times Index* early in a research project is to find the exact date of an event, to check proper names, and to get the gist of what *The New York Times* printed about it at the time and subsequently. Then the research trail can lead in several directions, such as:

(1) to the back files of *The New York Times* itself, whether in bound volumes or on microfilm, to read the articles for which the *Index* gives date, page and column;

(2) to the back files of other newspapers, especially those published in the city where the event occurred, in which coverage is likely to be more thorough than that in *The New York Times*;

(3) to other periodicals, such as magazines, learned society journals and newsletters, likely to have referred to the event.

In consulting other newspapers, the difference between morning and afternoon papers, and between time zones, may affect the date. For example, a Supreme Court ruling issued in Washington at noon on Monday would be covered in P.M. papers from coast to coast that same day. But it would be printed and indexed in *The New York Times* on Tuesday A.M.

Now See:
    Wall Street Journal Index (p. 52)
    The Times (of London) Index (p. 52)
    Readers' Guide to Periodical Literature (below)

Readers' Guide to Periodical Literature

The *Readers' Guide to Periodical Literature* (which I call *Readers' Guide* for convenience) is the best single source from which to find references to current and past magazine and journal articles, which the researcher can then locate in libraries and elsewhere. *Readers' Guide* is most useful as a quick way of answering three kinds of questions:

1. What articles on a given *subject* were published in general magazines in a specific period?

2. What articles by a certain *writer* were published in that time?

3. Exactly where (what magazine and issue) can I find an article to which I have been referred, without a complete citation?

The *Readers' Guide* indexes the articles in about 180 general and nontechnical periodicals, all published in the United States. Author and subject entries are combined in one alphabetical index, and each entry gives all necessary information for finding the article in the magazines: author, title, name of periodical (abbreviated), volume number, pages and date.

Many libraries keep bound volumes of *Readers' Guide* (which are bound in dark green) going back to its start in 1900. Since 1965 each volume covers one year; before that (1900–65), two to five years were in one volume. For the current year since publication of the last bound volume, the library usually keeps paperbound copies of semimonthly, monthly and quarterly issues loose in a box adjoining the bound volumes.

CAUTION:

Readers' Guide does not index all general and nontechnical magazines. Therefore, some articles on important subjects by writers of stature cannot be found in *Readers' Guide* — because the magazines in which they appeared were not covered by the indexers. Examples in 1979: *Playboy*, *Rolling Stone*, and the widely circulated Sunday newspaper supplement *Parade*. Each volume of *Readers' Guide* lists the publications indexed at that time but there is no convenient way to find which magazines of wide circulation were *not* indexed. You must compile your own list and search them separately.

The *Abridged Readers' Guide*, designed for use in school libraries, indexes about 60 publications and is widely used in secondary schools. Check to make sure that you have picked up the right version — they look much alike.

Now See:
  Periodical Indexes: the Two Levels (below)
  Know the Reference Book Catalogs (p. 49)
  Pre-1900 Periodical Indexes (p. 50)
  The "At-the-Bindery" Gap (p. 43)
  Services from Periodicals (p. 112)

Periodical Indexes: the Two Levels

See First:
  Readers' Guide to Periodical Literature (p. 28)

For comprehensive research in magazine articles the *Readers' Guide* is insufficient, because it is largely concerned with general magazines and covers relatively few specialized publications. To find articles in the latter, one should use one or more other indexes covering specialized magazines and journals in a broad field. Listed below are nine other indexes that divide among them the main areas of human concern with relatively few gaps, though there is some overlapping. Because they are all produced by the same publishing house that publishes the *Readers' Guide* (H. W. Wilson Company) the indexes follow a common system, which makes it easy for the user to go from one to the other. Caution: five are indexed by author and subject; four are indexed by subject only.

The H. W. Wilson Company does publish a few other specialized indexes, but the nine listed here are the most generally useful guides to articles in specialized periodicals. The field covered by each is suggested by its name:

Applied Science & Technology Index: covers about 300 periodicals, started in 1958. Before that date see its predecessor, the *Industrial Arts Index*, started in 1913.

Art Index: covers about 150 periodicals, started in 1929.

Biological & Agricultural Index: covers about 190 periodicals, has appeared under this title since 1964. Before that date see its predecessor, *Agricultural Index*, which was started in 1916.

Business Periodicals Index: covers about 270 periodicals, started in 1958. Before that date see its predecessor, *Industrial Arts Index*, started in 1913.

Education Index: covers about 330 periodicals, as well as proceedings, yearbooks, bulletins and monographic series published in Canada, Britain and the United States. Started in 1929.

General Science Index: covers about 90 general science periodicals, started in July 1978.

Humanities Index: covers more than 250 periodicals, started in 1974 under this title. Before that date see its predecessor, the *Social Sciences & Humanities Index* (1965–1974), and its predecessor, the *International Index*, which was published from 1907 to 1965.

Index to Legal Periodicals: covers about 375 legal periodicals, yearbooks, annual institutes and annual reviews of work in a given field, published in the United States, Canada, Great Britain, Ireland, Australia and New Zealand. Started in 1908.

Social Sciences Index: covers more than 260 periodicals, started in 1974 under this title. For earlier issues see *Humanities Index* (above).

INDEX TO LEGAL PERIODICALS 1976–1977

DIVORCE and separation

Avoiding self-incrimination in marriage dissolution proceedings. J. G. Reynolds. Fla B J 50: 528-31 N '76

Award of attorney's fees in divorce litigation in Texas. Houston L Rev 13:1016-40 Jl '76

Balance sheet liabilities: divorce, maritals, and their agreements. H. E. Solomon. NYU Inst Fed Taxation 35:1315-56 '77

Behind the law of divorce: a modern perspective. F. Bates. Man L J 7:39-55 '76

Boundaries of the divorce lawyer's role. B. W. Callner. Family L Q 10:389-98 Wint '77

Caribbean divorce for Americans: useful alternative or obsolescent institution? Cornell Int L J 10:116-33 D '76

Children of divorce. H. L. Bass. Tr Law Q 11: 54-61 Wint '75

Chronique de droit familial. A.-F. Bisson, F. Héloine. Rev Générale de Droit 5:333-82 '74

Civil procedure—rule 15(b)—amendment of pleadings to conform to evidence. Wake Forest L Rev 12:405-22 Summ '76

Community property—for apportionment of community business where appreciation is attributable to the husband's efforts after separation, the corporate entity may be disregarded if justified by the facts. Santa Clara L Rev 16:682-90 Summ '76

Community property in a common law jurisdiction: a seriously neglected area of the law. Washburn L J 16:77-101 Fall '76

Constitutional law—equal protection—constitutionality of divorce durational residency statute—mootness—maintenance of class action after mooting of named representative's claim.

Home is where I hang my div ical appraisal of Sosna v. Io B. R. Cromley. Calif Weste Summ '76

Husband's recovery of person atter judicial separation. La Summ '76

Impact of the revolution in Ge on antenuptial agreements. Wint '77

Initial interview with a div Barrett. Prac Law 23:75-86 J

Is a Louisiana wife liable f taxes on income earned by ing a judgment of separati 23:98-121 Wint '77

Jurisdiction in divorce and cor J. J. Sampson. Tex Tech Summ '76

Justice for the poor? A loo counsel for indigents in NY L S L Rev 22:87-102 '76

Law of child support in Geo Family L 14:464-75 '75-'76

Marital status and eligibility tory income benefits: a his D. Rompauer. Wash L Rev 5

Matrimonial property entitl Quebec conflicts of law. D. fication du régime des biens international privé québécoi Gill L J 22:315-20, 658-65

Milton as prophet: the divorc temporary divorce laws. H J   9-81 Ap '77

N   roach t

It is useful to consult periodicals at both levels — the general and the specialized. In most cases the researcher should first consult *Readers' Guide* for references in general circulation magazines. Only after that should he consult one or more of the nine specialized indexes, in order to find more detailed material written for the specialized readership. General circulation magazines such as *American Heritage* and *Saturday Review* frequently carry articles and illustrations of the highest quality, written by leading authorities, and benefiting from good editing. Broad conclusions and summaries clear to laymen are usually plainly stated. Specialized magazines and professional journals, on the other hand, are strong on detail and documentation, but are frequently obscurely written, poorly edited and not illustrated. Articles in both kinds of magazine are useful in research.

There is some overlap between the coverage of *Readers' Guide* and the other indexes. For instance, *Harvard Business Review* is

BUSINESS PERIODICALS INDEX

DIVORCE
Controlling the tax effects of transfers of life insurance or annuities in divorces. S. M. Harris and R. B. Rayikoff. J Taxation 47:92-6 Ag '77
Dealing the tax man out of a divorce. J. R. Dorfman. tab Money 6:81-2+ Je '77
Divorce; banishing guilt [Britain] Economist 265:25 N 19 '77
How not to dispose of property in a marital settlement. Practical Accountant 10:71 Jl '77
Ninth circuit reaffirms state law as the final arbiter of marital status. J Taxation 47:57 Jl '77
Pensions land in divorce court. Bus W p 104+ N 7 '77
Tax effects in divorce planning. P. J. Harmelink and N. E. Shurtz. CPA J 47:27-32 O '77
Who gets what in a divorce. R. Lavoie. il tab Money 7:66-9 Ap '78
Who is the surviving spouse in divorce and remarriage cases? a review of Spalding, Steffke and Goldwater. C. E. Wilkinson. Trusts & Estates 116:784-8 D '77
    See also
Alimony

Specialized indexes to periodicals provide references in hundreds of magazines and journals that are not covered by the Readers' Guide to Periodical Literature.

indexed both in *Readers' Guide* and in the *Business Periodicals Index;* and *Scientific American* is indexed in *Readers' Guide*, in *Applied Science & Technology Index* and in *General Science Index.* The vast majority of periodicals are covered by only one index, however. And with only few exceptions, they are published in the United States.

One should remember that the dividing lines between these indexes follow the subject matter of the *periodical* — not the subject matter of the particular *article.* Thus, an article on the education of engineers appearing in *Engineering* magazine would be found in the *Applied Sciences & Technology Index* (which indexes *Engineering* magazine) — not in the *Education Index.*

Only the largest of the city and university libraries subscribe to all the specialized indexes published by Wilson, so you may have to search for special libraries that carry the indexes you need. And you may have to search even farther for libraries that carry some of the specialized magazines to which the index entries refer you.

Now See:
   Know the Reference Book Catalogs (p. 49)
   The "At-the-Bindery" Gap (p. 43)
   Finding the Right Library (p. 17)
   Finding Special Libraries in Your City (p. 22)
   Services from Periodicals (p. 112)

Help at the Bookstore

Your neighborhood bookstore can be a help in research, especially when it is closer at hand than the library. Aside from the fact that experienced booksellers know their merchandise and can put their hands on a given title fast, they always keep certain reference books to help them order and sell books — and you can use these to advantage. On request the bookstore clerk will usually produce them for your inspection. They are:

1. *Subject Guide to Books in Print.* This annual lists more than 423,000 book titles currently available from 6,000 U.S. book publishers, indexed under 62,000 subject headings with numerous cross references. Here you can find in one place a list of all books *now on sale* (the publishing industry uses the term "in print") under a particular subject. By cross-checking the list of books in *Subject Guide* against your own bibliography compiled from libraries and elsewhere, you can determine what other current

VENDUES
see Auctions

VENEERS AND VENEERING
see also Plywood
Hobbs, Harry J. Veneering Simplified. (Illus.). 1976. 6.95 (ISBN 0-684-14544-8). Scribner
Villiard, Paul. A Manual of Veneering. (Illus.). 6.00 (ISBN 0-8446-5253-9). Peter Smith.
A Manual of Veneering. (Illus.). 1975. pap. 2.50 (ISBN 0-486-23217-4). Dover.

VENERATION OF SAINTS
see Saints-Cultus

VENEREAL DISEASES
see also Hygiene, Sexual; Lymphogranuloma Venereum; Syphilis; Treponematosis
Allison, Samuel D. & Johnson, June. VD Manual for Teachers. 4.95 (ISBN 0-87523-077-6). Emerson.
American Alliance for Health, Physical Education, & Recreation. Teacher's Handbook on Venereal Disease Education. 1965 pap. 2.75x (244-07710). AAHPER
Bender, Stephen J. Venereal Disease. 2nd ed. (Contemporary Topics in Health Science Ser.). 1975. pap. 1.95x (ISBN 0-697-07346-7). Wm C Brown.
Bibliography of Yaws: 1905-1962. (Eng, Fr, & Rus.). 1963. pap. 3.60 (ISBN 92-4-052003-1). World Health.
Blanzaco, Andre. VD: Facts You Should Know. LC 78-120168 (Illus.). (gr. 7-12). 1970. 6.75 (ISBN 0-688-41487-7); PLB 6.48 (ISBN 0-688-51487-1). Lothrop.
Brasch, Walter M. & Cox, Robert K. The Plain Truth About VD. 1978. pap. 5.95 (ISBN 0-89554-001-0). Brasch & Brasch.
Brooks, George F., et al, eds. Immunobiology of Neisseria Gonorrhoeae. (Illus.). 1978. text ed. 15.00 (ISBN 0-914826-18-2). Am Soc Microbio.
Brooks, Stewart M. The V. D. Story. LC 78-162704. (Illus.) 1971. 7.95 (ISBN 0-498-07934-1). A S Barnes.
- The V. D. Story: Medicine's Battle Against the Scourge of Venereal Disease. (Quality Paperback No. 252). (Illus.). 1973. pap. 1.95 (ISBN 0-8226-0252-0). Littlefield.
Brown, William J., et al. Syphilis & Other Venereal Diseases. LC 77-88803. (Vital & Health Statistics Monographs, American Public Health Association). 1970. 8.00x (ISBN 0-674-86122-1). Harvard U Pr.
Busch, Phyllis S. What About VD. LC 75-45147. (Illus.). (gr. 7 up). 1976. 6.95g (Four Winds). Schol Bk Serv.
Catterall, R. D. A Short Textbook of Venereology. 2nd ed. LC 73-21370. (Illus.) 1975. 9.75 (ISBN 0-397-58139-4) Lippincott.
Catterall, R. D., ed. Sexually Transmitted Diseases. 1976. 19.75 (ISBN 0-12-164150-3). Acad Pr.
- Venereology for Nurses. (Modern Nursing Ser.). 1964. pap. 4.00 (ISBN 0-87488-867-0). Med Exam
Chiappa, Joseph A & Forish, Joseph J. The VD Book. LC 77-018796-6, Hol
Deschin, Celia S. 13417. (Person Ser.). (gr. 7 up).

Hubbard, Charles W. Family Planning Education. 2nd ed. LC 76-14449. (Illus.). 1977 pap. text ed. 6.95 (ISBN 0-8016-2298-0) Mosby.
Hyde, Margaret O. VD: The Silent Epidemic. 5.95 (ISBN 0-07-031637-6); PLB 6.95 (ISBN 0-07-031638-4) McGraw.
Johnson, Eric W. V. D. 1973. 6.95 (ISBN 0-397-31447-7). Lippincott.
- V. D. Venereal Disease and What You Should Do About It. new and revised ed. (Illus.). (gr. 5-12) 1978. 6.95 (ISBN 0-397-31811-1). Lippincott.
Jones, Kenneth L., et al. VD. (Illus.). 1974. pap. text ed. 5.95x (ISBN 0-06-043421-X, HarpC). Har-Row.
Kieth, Louis & Brittain, Jan. Sexually Transmitted Diseases. Wells, John P., ed. Yuzpe, A. A., tr. from Fr. (Illus.). 1978. 6.75x. Creative Infomatics
Kimmig, Joseph & Janner, Michael. Frieboes-Schonfeld Color Atlas of Dermatology. Goldschmidt, Herbert, tr. LC 66-16253. (Illus.). 1966. 79.50 (ISBN 0-7216-3900-3). Saunders.
King, A. Venereal Diseases. 3rd ed. 1975. 30.00 (ISBN 0-683-04625-X). Williams & Wilkins.
Klingbeil, Reinhold. VD Is Not for Me. (Better Living Ser.). 1976. pap. 0.75. Southern Pub.
Kramer-Greene, Judith. Venereal Disease Bibliography for 1974. 1976. 15.00 (ISBN 0-87875-080-0). Whitston Pub.
- - Venereal Disease Bibliography for 1975. 1977. 25.00 (ISBN 0-87875-097-5). Whitston Pub.
Lasagna, Louis. The VD Epidemic: How It Started, Where It's Going, & What to Do About It. LC 74-29475. 1975. 12.50x (ISBN 0-87722-041-7). Temple U Pr.
Llewellyn-Jones, Derek. Sex & V. D. 1975. 6.95 (ISBN 0-571-10482-7); pap. 2.95 (ISBN 0-571-10483-5). Faber & Faber.
Lynch, P. & Epstein, Stephan. Burckhardt's Atlas & Manual of Dermatology & Venereology. 3rd ed. (Illus.). 1976. 42.00 (ISBN 0-683-01134-0). Williams & Wilkins.
Mali, J. W., ed. Current Problems in Dermatology, Vol. 3. 1970. 32.00 (ISBN 3-8055-0484-5). S Karger.
Morton, Barbara. VD: A Guide for Nurses & Counselors. 1976. pap. 8.95 (ISBN 0-316-58530-0). Little.
Morton, R. S. Sexual Freedom & Venereal Disease. (Contemporary Issues Ser: No. 5). 1971. text ed. 10.00x (ISBN 0-7206-0411-7). Humanities.
- - Venereal Diseases. (Illus., Orig.) 1966. pap. 1.50 (ISBN 0-14-020819-4, Pelican) Penguin.
Morton, Robert S. & Harris, John R. Recent Advances in Sexually Transmitted Diseases. (Illus.). 1975. text ed. 35.00x (ISBN 0-443-01156-7). Churchill.
Neumann, Hans & Simmons, Sylvia. The Straight Story on V. D. (Orig.). 1973. pap. 1.25 (ISBN 0-446-76354-3). Warner Bks.
Nicholas, Leslie. How to Avoid Social Diseases:

W. Alton Jor
Nongono
Oculogeni
Derek & I
1977. 14.0(
WHO Expert C,
Infections, Is
(Technical R
Rus, & Spar
120262-9)
Williams, Eliza
Burnes, Al
(Illus., Ori
(ISBN 0-8
Wisdom, An
(Year Bo
25.00 (I
World Dir-
Centre
Intern
Respec
Seamer
Disease
050001-
Young, Elea
(Career C
text ed. 4
VENESECTI
see Bloodletting
VENETIC LAN
Hempl, George. M
1 vol. Anderson
Vol. 1. The Ge
Writing; Pt. 1,
Vol. 3. Three
Language of
Etruscan; F
ed. pap te
AMS Pr
VENEZUEI
Carpenter, A
of Vene.
South A.
PLB 7.70
Conference
10-11, 1t
Progress.
(ISBN 0-
Dalton, L. Ve
bdg. 34.95
Dauxion-Lavay-
& Political D
Margarita, &
1820 ed. 19.5(
Negro U Pr.
Fergusson, Erna.
Bookbindery.
James, Henry. R·
Service. LC
(Illus.). 197
(ISBN 0-2·
Nesbitt, L.
Orinoc
Arde·

books there are that you had not known about. As a practical matter, consulting the *Subject Guide to Books in Print* should be one of the first steps in building up a bibliography.

2. *Books in Print*. A companion to the above, this annual comes in two sets — one listing authors alphabetically, and the other listing titles. In them you can find quickly all titles in print by a given author, or pin down the author of a book of which you know the title.

3. *Paperbound Books in Print*. This index of current paperbound books appears twice a year, giving you a way to find and buy your own paperbound copy of a book you require. PBIP lists paperbound books by author, title and subject area. Division by subjects is not in such specific detail as in *Subject Guide* (above); there are about 130 subject areas, and within these the user must search.

Reference libraries generally have copies of these three aids to book finding, but they are often kept in a place convenient to the staff, rather than where readers can readily find and use them. In bookstores they are almost always handy for sales people and for customers. All three are published by the R. R. Bowker Company, 1180 Avenue of the Americas, New York, N.Y. 10036.

A Low-Cost Home Reference Collection

In steering a course between wasting time and wasting money, I have found that it pays to buy a certain number of inexpensive reference books so that I can have them right on my desk, and to consult others in the library. Of course, each researcher discovers his own needs and use patterns, and each buys reference materials of particular value to him. But for general use I suggest this short list of reference books:

1. *The World Almanac*. Published annually for a century, this is the standard American book of facts from which others (such as the *Information Please Almanac* and *The New York Times Encyclopedic Almanac*) were derived. Sold at newsstands in soft cover, it is the best available compilation of specific information in many fields, and has been at the right hand of thousands of newspaper editors for decades. The strength of the *World Almanac* lies in its excellent index, which includes both general subject headings and specific names. Every house and office should have this time-saving reference book. So should every student, from high school through the doctoral degree candidate.

2. *Congressional Directory.* Published after every biennial Congressional election, and revised semiannually between elections, the *Congressional Directory* is the definitive guide to the resources of American federal government. Most space is devoted to Congress and its committees, but there are also lists of federal courts and judges, and of agencies and officers of the Executive branch of government. From the Executive branch pages you can find name, address, telephone number, organizational structure and public information officer of an agency from which you seek help in research.

After a Congressional election and pending the appearance of a new edition (in late spring in odd-number years), you can clip a newspaper or magazine summary of election results and use it as a temporary correction sheet, at least for the names of new members of Congress.

Now See:
   Government as an Information Source (p. 62)
   Government Printing Office (p. 65)
   Your Congressman Can Help (p. 68)

3. *United States Government Organization Manual.* A companion to the *Congressional Directory* (described above), this annual (in soft and hard cover) goes into much greater detail on each agency of the Executive branch of federal government. It includes material on the origin and authority of each agency, from which you can determine whether or not a given agency is the right one for you to query.

Now See:
   Government as an Information Source (p. 62)
   Government Printing Office (p. 65)
   Your Congressman Can Help (p. 68)

4. *Statistical Abstract of the United States.* Published annually since 1879, this collection of definitive statistical tables is prepared by the U.S. Bureau of the Census and is sold by the Government Printing Office. It includes the most generally useful data collected both by government agencies and by nongovernment agencies and associations. Subjects range widely over demography, social statistics, economics, finance, business and population. Time span covered by the statistical series varies; some were begun in this century, whereas others extend back into Colonial times.

Now See:
Government Printing Office (p. 65)

5. *Facts About the Presidents* by Joseph Nathan Kane (H. W. Wilson Company). This is highly useful for quick reference to events and dates in U.S. history, organized by Presidential administrations. Supplements appear as new Presidents come to office.

6. *National Geographic Society Maps.* Rather than invest in an expensive bound atlas that may become outdated by boundary changes or the formation of new states, I collect the loose, folded maps inserted every few months in the *National Geographic Magazine.* Over the years this collection has become my self-updating atlas, measuring six inches across as the folded maps stand on the shelf. I bind together the maps of each continent with a rubber band, and can easily find the map I need within a minute. For accuracy of place names, clarity and precision in cartography, and quality of printing the National Geographic Society maps are unsurpassed in the United States.

7. *Reference Books: A Brief Guide,* published by Enoch Pratt Free Library, Baltimore. This softcover guide to reference books is a "must" for any serious researcher. Read the description of it in *The Best Guide to Reference Books* (p. 24).

8. *Your college or university alumni directory* (if any). The great value of an alumni directory is that it helps you find people whom you knew in student days, who are now in places or situations where they can assist you in research. Some may be experts in fields where you can use friendly guidance. Others can serve as guides to their localities, where you may have no other personal connections. But whether or not you were well acquainted as students, the old school tie can frequently serve as a friendly connecting link between you as the researcher and your fellow alumnus as a source of information.

Now See:
Information Networks: Alumni Offices (p. 79)

9. *Your trade or professional directory* (if any). There are hundreds of directories and annuals published for the reference use of people engaged in the same general business or professional activity. Sometimes these books are known as "the Bible of the

industry." Depending on price and frequency of use, an individual can decide for himself whether it pays to buy his own copy or to use it in a library. Many directories and annuals carry paid advertising, which helps the publisher to bring the price down and gain a greater circulation. When undertaking research for the first time in a given business or professional field, you should become familiar at once with the standard reference work (or works) and acquire it if need be.

Now See:
Search Out the Trade Press (p. 89)

Getting Library Discards for Yourself

Many libraries, especially well-financed company libraries, make it a practice to discard superseded reference books when a new edition reaches them. They may do so both because of lack of shelf space and because they are interested in current information only. However, the next-to-latest edition of most serial reference books, particularly annuals, can be highly useful to the individual researcher, because most of the information in them is sufficiently up to date for his purposes.

It is therefore well worth the time and trouble to make contact with a cooperative librarian in charge of a special library with a policy of discarding superseded editions, and arrange that the books be given to you instead of being thrown out. When one considers the price of such reference books as *Who's Who in America*, *Who's Who in Finance and Industry*, and the *Encyclopedia of Associations*, to name a few, cementing a friendly relationship with a librarian to whom you offer carry-away service is most advantageous.

Biographical Research: Basic Steps

Tracking down information about people, living or dead, is a fascinating branch of research, but you can waste a great deal of time if you don't go about it right. I have found it most productive to go first to the most general sources of information, and later to the more specific sources. I follow this order lest, in my desire to get down to particulars, I miss something important about the subject. Among the first sources to consult are these:

1. *Who's Who in America*, the standard biographical dictionary published every other year, beginning in 1899. This is the best

single guide to living notable Americans. But the user should remember that (a) entries are based on questionnaires filled out by the biographees, so no information that the subject considers derogatory is included; and (b), some notables do not fill out questionnaires. In some of these cases the editors may research and write an original biographical sketch if they believe that an omission would impair the usefulness of the book for reference.

The publisher, Marquis Who's Who, Inc., also publishes four regional Who's Who books covering U.S. notables in the East, the Midwest, the West, and the South and Southwest. If you do not find your subject in Who's Who in America, check the regional books next. Marquis Who's Who, Inc., publishes a dozen other biographical directories of the Who's Who in—————— type, covering people in various fields of work and certain past periods, and it publishes a name index to the biographees in all its directories. It pays to ask a librarian for the complete list from this publisher.

Who's Who (that's the full title), published annually since 1849, is the British counterpart of the American book. Be careful to specify which one you want in a library; the similarity of titles and of appearance often causes confusion between the two.

Who Was Who in America summarizes the records of Americans now dead. You can usually find more information by referring to an old volume of Who's Who in America published when the subject was alive.

2. Current Biography, published by H. W. Wilson Company since 1940, is the next best general source of information on important contemporary personalities; and on those now dead who were written about when still living. The index in each volume extends back to the start of the decade only. (For instance, the 1966 volume index covers 1961–66.) However, a Current Biography Cumulated Index covers the years 1940–70, and your library may have acquired this separate index. Some subjects whose careers spanned more than one decade have been written about more than once (example, Dwight D. Eisenhower), so for information on them check the indexes with care. The great value of Current Biography lies in its editorial independence of its subjects. Each biographical article, averaging about 2,000 words, is written by the Wilson staff from information gathered from a variety of sources, both critical and favorable, rather than from the biographee alone. A short bibliography is supplied, permitting the researcher to locate further material on the subject.

3. *Encyclopaedia Britannica*, and other encyclopedias. It hardly needs stating here that encyclopedias such as *Britannica* (as well as *Americana, Chambers's, Collier's, Compton's,* etc.) contain many biographical articles primarily on people now dead. What researchers frequently overlook is that *Britannica* ends each biographical article with a bibliography, from which you can quickly obtain references to the best (in the view of *E.B.*) books on the subject. For brief identification of names and people, and for condensed biographical information, the one-volume *Columbia Encyclopedia* is a great time-saver. It is often open on a stand in the library reference room.

4. *Card Catalog in a Reference Library.* A standard step early in biographical research is to check the card catalog of a reference library under the subject's name, to find whatever books about that person, or written by him, are on hand. To find additional current books about or by the subject, books not in your library, consult *Subject Guide to Books in Print* (see p. 32), considering the person as a subject indexed by last name. Books by or about living people, especially those in politics, sports and entertainment, are pouring from the presses today. It therefore pays to look to see if one has been published on a young, newly prominent person.

5. *Obituaries.* Newspaper and magazine obituaries are good sources of biographical material about people who were not national notables. The key to all obituaries is finding the date of death, then going to the files of local newspapers in the library, as well as to publications of organizations with which the subject was connected (clubs, unions, professional societies, etc.).

The New York Times Index (see p. 26) is valuable in determining the death date of people of stature, even though they were not of national renown or New York figures. In 1970 *The New York Times* published *The New York Times Obituaries Index* as a key to finding the right obituary among more than 350,000 published in that newspaper since 1858.

Researchers should not accept obituaries as gospel truth. They are just useful guides to the facts, which the reader must follow and check. Newspaper obituaries are usually written against a demanding daily deadline, and the writers must rely on distraught family members for much of their information on the recently deceased. The general outline is usually right, but the specifics are frequently incorrect. Magazine obituaries, which are written more slowly, are usually more reliable than those in daily papers.

6. *Periodical Indexes.* Biographical material, ranging from the most general kind of magazine article to the most specific and parochial, can be found in the *Readers' Guide to Periodical Literature* (see p. 28) and in the other more specialized indexes to magazines, published by the H. W. Wilson Co. (see p. 29). The same is true of *The New York Times Index* (see p. 26). For a general framework you can profitably look first under the subject's name in *Readers' Guide* or *The New York Times Index;* but much more biographical detail can be extracted from the specialized journals and magazines in the fields of the subject's life and work. This is particularly the case with obituary articles in learned society journals. These are often written by a close colleague who knew the subject more intimately than any journalist, and may often write things into the obituary that had not been published before.

Now See:
Biographical Reference: a Few Useful Books (p. 54)

Professional Tips on Note-Taking

Everyone has taken notes on what he has read, seen or heard, but there are good ways and bad ways to take notes. Here are a number of tips that can help you avoid errors and loss of time.

1. *Thoroughness.* Don't make your notes so cryptic that some time later you will be in doubt as to exactly what the notes mean. Avoid writing notes so brief that you alone can understand them. If you use symbols or abbreviations, write down a key to their meanings for later reference. Do not rely too much on memory because it fails us all at times.

2. *System.* Organize your notes into a system according to your intended *use* of the material — not according to its source. Do record the source of every note, because you may want to return to it later to check for accuracy or to pick up more material. I have found it best to put notes on only one subject on a sheet of paper, and to use a fresh sheet for material on a different subject. Then I am free to shuffle the sheets around in order to get them in the order I want for use.

It is most convenient to use entire sheets rather than small slips of paper, which have an annoying way of being overlooked or lost. (The extra cost of paper is minor, and well worth the convenience.) Another advantage is that additional material on the same subject can be added later to the same sheet. If a given note can be used under more than one heading, either place a cross-file note ("See Also") under the second heading to avoid copying the note, or copy the note, place it under the second heading, and mark it with a reminder that you have placed the first copy elsewhere. In this way you will be reminded that the note is in two places, and you can avoid repeating yourself when you finally decide where to use the material.

3. *Bibliographical notes.* Note down the full data on books consulted, or sought, in research to avoid confusion with other books having similar titles, or different editions, or authors with the same or similar names. A bibliographical note such as: "*History of Europe*, by Smith" is worthless. There are too many library catalog cards starting with the words "History of Europe," and countless authors with the last name Smith. However, after you have identified a book with precision in your notes you can best save time by referring to it by the surname of the author, because book titles are longer than surnames and there are more similarities among titles.

When first consulting a book, note down the author, title, city of publication, publisher and year of publication. These are the required items in a formal bibliography. If you write them down once when the book is in your hands you can save the time of chasing after these details later. (I have never heard a convincing explanation of the need for the city of publication of a nationally known publisher, such as McGraw-Hill, but academics persist in asking for it.)

When working in a library where the 3" by 5" call slips (order slips) are returned to me with the books when they are brought from the stacks, I have found it convenient to keep the call slips as my primary bibliographical notes. I file them alphabetically by author, put a clip or rubber band around the call slips for each project on which I am working, and store them in a shoe box (ladies' size). On each slip I make a very brief note of evaluation, such as: "Nothing here," or "Excellent."

4. *Negative results.* You should note down negative results — failure to find anything worth noting — from a source, as an aide-mémoire for later use. Otherwise, the absence of any notes from a potential research source may lead you to investigate it a second time.

5. *Mechanics of note-taking.* Whenever possible, take notes on a typewriter rather than by hand. Typing is faster, and there is no

difficulty reading your notes later. If your library permits the use of a silent portable, the investment is well worth it.

I have found cards unsatisfactory for note-taking for two reasons: (a) you run out of space quickly on one side of a card; and (b), cards are more cumbersome than sheets of paper to insert into the typewriter.

Take notes on only *one side* of a sheet of paper. Many a backside note has been lost in the shuffle.

Clean out your notes regularly; remove outdated items and those found later to be incorrect. It is better to have a compact set of useful notes than to lose your useful pages among a mass of notes that you will never use again.

Public Relations Sources

Public relations people and offices can be of great help to the researcher. They go under various names — public relations (often PR for short), publicity, public information (the term used in government), press relations and, in embassies, press attaché. Whatever the name, these are the people and offices whose job it is to supply information to the press and the public on behalf of an organization, institution or individual.

In recent years the PR function has become so important in the United States that in many cases the person best equipped to supply information about an institution is the PR director — not the president or chief executive officer. Most academics have not accepted this fact, so very few professors tell students how to use the PR network. One reason is that there is an academic prejudice against PR sources as unscholarly. This prejudice is beside the point, because no one seeking information from a PR source should park his critical faculties at the door. He should be as careful in accepting what they tell him as he would be about statements he reads in a journal article or a book.

This caution is in order when dealing with the public information officer of a university or a government agency, just as it is with the PR man of a manufacturing company or an airline. It is the researcher's job to screen out what is valid and factual from that which is distorted, inflated or untrue. If the researcher recognizes that he should count on the PR source for only certain parts of the story, and if he can discount the rest, then the PR source can save him a great deal of time in assembling those valid parts. In sum, do not overlook the service that a PR source can give, but always remember that he is paid by a special interest.

When making the first contact with an organization I have got around terminology differences by asking for "the public relations director, or whoever acts in that capacity." This approach usually gets results. A second step, particularly with large companies, is to find out whether it does its own PR work or employs an outside PR agency. If the latter, you should find out which public relations agency represents the company, and then find the *account executive* at the agency who is responsible for that client.

The PR agency will usually supply the inquiring student, writer or anyone else with information because doing so is evidence of work performed on the client's behalf. If, in approaching an agency, you indicate how you intend to use the client's name in a favorable way, so much the better. Agency people willingly give their time to answer questions because that is what they are paid to do. A PR person can save you much effort by supplying reports, texts, statistics, pictures and bibliographies.

In the case of a big company or institution frequently no one outside its national headquarters can tell you whether a PR agency represents it, and if so, which one. If you cannot find out easily through local company sources, consult *O'Dwyer's Directory of Public Relations Firms*, Jack O'Dwyer, editor; J. R. O'Dwyer Co., Inc., 271 Madison Avenue, New York, N.Y. 10016. Listings in this annual directory are broken down by client name, by type of PR firm and by city. A companion annual, *O'Dwyer's Directory of Corporate Communications*, is organized by companies and gives details of their internal PR staff. Because PR is a fast-changing business, it is always smart to double-check discreetly to make certain that a given company is still a client of an agency listed in the O'Dwyer annual, or that a person named as the public relations director is still in the same position. General information about public relations may be obtained from the Information Center of the Public Relations Society of America, 845 Third Avenue, New York, N.Y. 10022.

The "At-the-Bindery" Gap

See First:
    Readers' Guide to Periodical Literature (p. 28)
    Periodical Indexes: the Two Levels (p. 29)

Libraries frequently remove from the shelves the issues of magazines that are one to two years old and send them out for binding in hardcover volumes. Unless the library keeps a second set of unbound issues for use during this "at-the-bindery" gap, there may be several weeks during which you would not have access to the issues. The most common practice is for magazines to be sent to the bindery when they are no longer current, and when copies covering the last full year can be left on the shelves.

To avoid fruitless trips to the library to consult magazines that are from one to three years old, you can ask the reference librarian to tell you whether the issues you need are on the shelves or at the bindery. Most librarians keep an accurate "at-the-bindery" list at the service desk, and can answer this query at once. But they rarely volunteer the information before you have spent your time looking for missing issues.

B. INTERMEDIATE TECHNIQUES

Access to Library Stacks

See First:
Finding the Right Library (p. 17)
Dealing with Librarians (p. 22)

Although reference libraries generally do not permit readers to roam at will in the stacks, they make exceptions for serious researchers whom they know and trust. Most libraries have formalized this by issuing a stack pass to a limited number of qualified readers who present convincing credentials. Gaining access to the stacks is of great value to the researcher in a library where books are cataloged and arranged by subject because:

1. You can often find the books you need more quickly by going to the shelves, than by filing call slips at the service desk and waiting for books to be delivered;

2. You can find additional useful books that you would not find from the card catalog; and,

3. You will sometimes find books you have ordered, but which stack attendants overlook because they are misplaced on the shelves.

All three of these statements have been proven many times in my own experience in the Library of Congress and elsewhere.

By consulting the subject heading in the library card catalog, you can find the call number under which books on that subject are listed and arranged on the shelves. You can fill out call slips for every book under that heading, send for them, examine them, and retain the most useful ones for study. But it is much more efficient to find the call number, then go to the place in the stacks where the books under that number are shelved, and examine them in place. It may be a dusty business, carried out under poor lighting. But it pays, because you can examine and reject a dozen books quickly and walk out to the reading room with two or three that you consider the best — in terms of recent publication date, quality of the index, illustrations, readable type, clarity of style and coverage of the subject.

A second advantage of stack-searching is that it permits you to search the adjoining shelves, where books on closely allied subjects (with slightly different call numbers) can be found. For instance, biographies of astronomers may adjoin histories of astronomy, technical books on astronomical instruments, and bound volumes of astronomy journals. Because these various classifications of book are close at hand, you may come upon useful material that you would not have found so readily by using the card catalog.

In a big reference library a book may be misshelved just a few places away from its correct numerical position, with the result that the stack attendant may not find it. He then reports "Not on Shelf" to the reader who ordered it. If the book is reported "Not on Shelf" on a second attempt another day, you can profitably take time to look for yourself in the stacks, close to where the book should be shelved. For one thing, your motivation is greater than the stack attendant's; and you may know something about the appearance of the book, and so recognize it more easily.

CAUTION:

If several books in the same subject field are reported as unavailable, ask the librarian to examine the file of checked-out books to see who has them. You may find that another reader is doing research in the same field, and has drawn out the books for which you are looking. If so, it is better to propose sharing the books rather than competing for use of them.

Know the Reference Book Catalogs

The best way to keep up with most useful general reference books and services, many of which are updated annually, is to read the latest catalogs of the companies that publish them. The two most important of these companies are the *R. R. Bowker Company*, 1180 Avenue of the Americas, New York, N.Y. 10036; and the *H. W. Wilson Company*, 950 University Avenue, Bronx, N.Y. 10452. The publicity or sales departments of both companies will send a catalog on request.

There are, in addition, a number of publishers specializing in reference materials in law, medicine, the natural sciences and others, but the number of titles they produce is far below those from *Bowker* and *Wilson*. Their lists will be familiar to the experienced librarian in a special library in those particular fields.

Bowker (since 1967 a subsidiary of the Xerox Corporation) and *Wilson* are the two giants of American reference book publishing. Both houses add to their lists by creating new titles and series to their lines, and *Bowker* also absorbs reference book series from other publishers. Because the price of their reference books is prohibitive for most private users, they sell largely to libraries. In virtually no area do *Bowker* and *Wilson* compete; they divide the library market between them, each producing the definitive book, series or service in a given sector of the reference field. *Bowker* concentrates, though not exclusively, on books of direct aid to librarians, rather than to readers in libraries. *Wilson* concentrates on indexes to periodicals.

Here are a few of the most useful reference books among some 300 titles described in the *Bowker* catalog: *American Library Directory, American Men and Women of Science, Audiovisual Market Place, Books in Print (Author–Title Index), Directory of American Scholars, Information Market Place, Paperbound Books in Print, Subject Collections, Subject Guide to Books in Print, Ulrich's International Periodicals Directory.*

Some of the most useful books described in the catalog of *Wilson* publications are: *Current Biography, Biography Index, 19th Century Readers' Guide to Periodical Literature, Readers' Guide to Periodical Literature,* and the more specialized indexes to periodical articles described in this book in *Periodical Indexes: the Two Levels* (p. 29). *Wilson* distributes a free pamphlet entitled *Cataloging and Indexing Services,* which is a highly useful explanatory addition to the catalog. Ask the company to send both to you.

Another reference materials publisher, newer than *Bowker* and *Wilson*, issues a catalog of value to the serious researcher. It is *Gale Research Company*, 1400 Book Tower, Detroit, Mich. 48226. I have found these five items on the *Gale* list of more than 60 titles most useful in my work: *Book Review Index, Contemporary Authors, Encyclopedia of Associations, Directory of Special Libraries and Information Centers, National Directory of Newsletters and Reporting Services.*

A fourth publisher of reference materials worth checking is Marquis Who's Who, Inc., 200 East Ohio Street, Chicago, Illinois 60611. Aside from the widely known *Who's Who in America* (see p. 37), Marquis produces more than 25 biographical directories of the *Who's Who* or *Who Was Who* type. It is therefore worth a researcher's trouble to ask at a bookstore or library for the latest list from this company to see whether it has produced a new biographical directory that can help in a research project. A time-saver, if your library has it, is the Marquis *Index to All Books.* It lists the names of about 280,000 biographees for whom sketches were contained in 14 current Marquis directories at the time the index was prepared, and shows in which directory they appeared.

The main purpose of having at hand your own up-to-date catalogs from *Bowker, Wilson, Gale* and *Marquis Who's Who* is to see exactly what your local libraries are being offered by these major reference book publishers. When they publish new titles you can find out about them — sometimes before your local library obtains them. By learning something about all these source materials from the catalogs, you know what to ask for in the library. You can also query libraries by telephone in order to find which has the exact reference works you want.

Now See:
Periodical Indexes: the Two Levels (p. 29)

Pre-1900 Periodical Indexes

See First:
Readers' Guide to Periodical Literature (p. 28)
Periodical Indexes: the Two Levels (p. 29)

There are two highly useful indexes for research into magazines published before the start of *Readers' Guide* in 1900, and before the start of the more specialized periodical indexes published by H. W. Wilson Company and described on pp. 29–32). They are

Poole's Index to Periodical Literature, which covers a century from 1802 to 1906, and the *Nineteenth Century Readers' Guide to Periodical Literature*, which covers the decade 1890–99.

1. *Poole's Index* does not list authors. It indexes articles under subject only; poems and stories are listed under titles. Its entries appear skimpy when compared to those in present-day indexes, but *Poole's* is the only subject index we have that covers most of the nineteenth century. Volume I covers 1802–81; Volumes 2–6 cover the years 1882–1906.

In 1970, the *Author Index for Poole's*, edited by C. Edward Wall, was published by Pierian Press (Box 1808, Ann Arbor, Mich. 48106). Because this author index is relatively new, many libraries that carry *Poole's Index* may not have acquired this valuable companion reference work. But you may find it at a large reference library nearby.

2. The *Nineteenth Century Readers' Guide to Periodical Literature*, published by H. W. Wilson, is something of a misnomer because this index covers only the decade of the nineties, rather than the nineteenth century. Articles in fifty-one periodicals are indexed by subject, author and illustrator. Poems and fiction are indexed by title. This work overlaps *Poole's* and improves on it. Further, it carries supplementary indexing forward into the twentieth century (as H. W. Wilson explains it) "in order to make the indexing complete for each title from 1890 to the time when it was added to the list of one of the other Wilson indexes."

Two Off-Beat Periodical Indexes

In deciding which periodicals to cover in the *Readers' Guide to Periodical Literature*, the H. W. Wilson Co. follows a somewhat conservative course in using a poll of its subscribers to determine whether to add a new magazine to its coverage. Most subscribers are librarians, who generally do not spend money on new periodicals for which there is not a widespread demand, or ones that may subject them to criticism by would-be library censors. Wilson therefore receives relatively few suggestions that the *Readers' Guide* add to its coverage new periodicals that are local in orientation, or those that express unorthodox and minority viewpoints, or those heavily slanted toward sex. As a result, a large number of such periodicals, and others, that grew to significant size and importance in the 1960s and 1970s are not indexed in the *Readers' Guide*. Two relatively new indexes have been established to help fill this void.

Founded in 1973 and covering 15 periodicals at that time, *Popular Periodical Index* (P.O. Box 739, Camden, N.J. 08102) by 1979 was covering 36 magazines not indexed by the *Readers' Guide.* Among them: *Columbia Journalism Review*, *Conservative Digest*, *Crawdaddy*, *Mother Jones*, *Playboy*, *Prevention*, *Rolling Stone* and *TV Guide.* Some of them are special-interest rather than general-interest magazines (e.g. *Down beat*) and some are regional, such as *Chicago*, *Connecticut* and *New West.* The fact that *Popular Periodical Index* was carried in more than 1,400 libraries in its fifth year of publication means it has become widely available to researchers.

The *Alternative Press Index* (P.O. Box 7229, Baltimore, Md. 21218) has been published since 1970, and is produced by the Alternative Press Center, 2958 Greenmount Avenue, Baltimore. The index covers more than 150 alternative and radical newspapers, magazines and journals which cover such topics as gay rights, minority rights, socialism, third world movements and the women's equality movement. Approximately 600 libraries subscribe to the index.

The researcher who uses the *Alternative Press Index* and *Popular Periodical Index* may find it difficult to follow up the index references he finds in them, because relatively few general libraries maintain back files of the periodicals they cover. For this reason, if he fails to find them in the appropriate special libraries, he may have to appeal to the publisher for back copies, or else locate an enthusiastic subscriber nearby who retains his old copies.

Indexes to the Wall Street Journal, The Times (of London) and Others

See First:
   The New York Times Index (p. 26)

Beyond *The New York Times Index*, other published indexes to daily newspapers in English that have been widely available in reference libraries for several years are those of the *Wall Street Journal* and *The Times* (of London). Further, a few libraries in North America carry the bound index to the *Glasgow Herald*, which dates back to 1906.

In the 1970s the Micro Photo Division of Bell & Howell (Old Mansfield Road, Wooster, Ohio 44691) undertook a major program of microfilming a great many American newspapers, and providing printed indexes to the current contents of a dozen or more major newspapers. Among the dailies indexed by Bell & Howell are: *American Banker, Chicago Tribune, Chicago Sun-Times, Christian Science Monitor, Denver Post, Detroit News, Houston Post, Los Angeles Times, New Orleans Times-Picayune, San Francisco Chronicle, Washington Post,* and ten U.S. newspapers aimed at a black readership. The interested researcher can ask a reference librarian if indexes to other papers have been issued recently, because Bell & Howell is actively striving to build its list. It remains to be seen how widely these newer newspaper indexes will be distributed among research libraries outside the metropolitan region where each is important.

The *Wall Street Journal Index* is particularly strong in references to business and financial news printed in the WSJ Monday through Friday (there are no Saturday and Sunday issues). This index has been published since 1958. Each of the bound annual volumes is divided into two parts: one lists articles under the names of companies, and the other comprises all references other than company names. You should therefore check both indexes in a volume — one under the company name and the other under key words or personal names.

Researchers who seek the index to *The Times*, the daily newspaper published in London, should be sure they get that one rather than *The New York Times Index*, because sometimes library assistants are confused by the similarity in name and appearance of these two indexes. The London newspaper and its index (the latter published since 1906) naturally center on British news. Because articles of interest to British readers embrace broad coverage of the British Commonwealth, the *London Times Index* has many entries on subjects not found in *The New York Times* and its index. *Palmer's Index to The Times*, not produced by the newspaper itself, sketchily covers the London paper's contents from 1790 to 1905.

Americans should be warned that the *London Times* method of indexing is different from that commonly followed in the United States. Here, particular names dominate an index; in London, the particular name is often a subordinate entry under a general subject heading. For instance, the New York index includes the name "Wilkins, Hubert," referring to an article on a contestant of that name who participated in the England-to-Australia air race of 1919. In the London index, however, "Wilkins" does not appear in the "W" entries. An article about him is found by looking first under "Aeronautics," then under "Contests," then under "England-to-Australia Race." More recently, the 1960 London index cites articles on the U.S. national tennis championships at Forest Hills, N.Y., first under "United States," which is a subheading under "Lawn Tennis." *The New York Times Index* carries all stories of that sport under one heading, "Tennis," in order of date.

Biographical Reference: a Few Useful Books

See First:
  Biographical Research: Basic Steps (p. 37)

There are so many published biographical reference materials that it would be futile to try to list one-tenth of them in this book. The few described below are selected because they are among the most widely distributed in libraries, and therefore the easiest to find, and because they are among the biographical source books of most general use. Researchers looking for limited biograpical facts will find that they offer fast answers. But those digging beneath the surface of things should consider these books only as useful aids at the start.

1. *Biography Index*, published by H. W. Wilson Co. since 1946 and described in the Wilson catalog (see p. 49). This is a highly useful index that brings together, under the subject's name, references to biographical material appearing in about 2,400 periodicals indexed in other Wilson indexes; in current books of biography in English; in obituaries; and in incidental biographical material from otherwise nonbiographical books. In brief, the editors of *Biography Index* have assembled many references, saving the researcher who uses the index a great deal of time. It is published quarterly, and bound in annual and in three-year cumulations.

2. *American Men and Women of Science* (the title before 1972 was *American Men of Science*), edited by Jaques Cattell Press, Tempe, Arizona, distributed by R. R. Bowker & Co., and described in the Bowker catalog (see p. 49). The 13th edition of this biographical reference set, covering well over 100,000 scientists, consists of seven volumes. Six of the volumes are devoted to biographical sketches of American and Canadian scientists active in these fields: biology; chemistry; consulting; medical and health sciences; physics, astronomy, mathematics, statistics and computer sciences; and social and behavioral sciences. The seventh volume is a geographic and discipline index.

Take special note of the volume on the social and behavioral sciences, which covers those active in economics, political science, psychology and sociology. Librarians and students often overlook this reference work because the title *American Men and Women of Science* has the misleading connotation of the natural sciences only.

3. *Directory of American Scholars*, edited by the Jaques Cattell Press, Tempe, Arizona, and distributed by the R. R. Bowker Co. (see reference to the Bowker catalog on p. 49). The 7th edition contains biographical material on some 40,000 scholars in four volumes, divided this way: Volume I, History; Volume II, English,

SCHLEICH, ALLAN M, b. Hastings, Minn, July 19, 24; m. 45; c. 4. ENGLISH HISTORY. A.B, Col. St. Thomas, 45; A.M, Univ. Chicago, 47; Ph.D, Univ. Nebr, 60. Assoc. prof. HIST, CREIGHTON UNIV, 46-65, PROF, 65-, CHMN. DEPT, 63- U.S.A.A.F, 42-44, 2nd Lt. AHA; Mediaeval Acad. Am; Am. Cath. Hist. Asn; Conf. Brit. Stud; Midwest Medi____ ____ _____ century England—John Bright; 17th century British Duke of Hamilton. Add: Dept. of History, Creighton NE 68178.

SCHLEICH, RUDOLF J, b. Dingolfing, Ger, May 11, 2(c. 5. MODERN EUROPEAN HISTORY. B.S. & N.Y. : Canisius Col, 50; M.A, State Univ. N.Y Buffalo, 52; F Vienna, 54-55; Ph.D.(hist), Fordham Univ, 68. Instr. (PA), 57-60, asst. prof, 60-67, assoc. prof, 67-71, P. & DEAN COL, 69-, chmn. dept, 68-69. U.S.A, 44-46. Acad. Deans; East. Asn. Col. Deans & Adv. Stud.(mer Early Christian era; 17th century Habsburg history; diplomacy. Add: Dept. of History, King's College, W

SCHLEIFER, JAMES THOMAS, b. Rochester, N.Y, No AMERICAN HISTORY. B.A, Hamilton Col. 64; M.A. Ph.D.(hist), 72. Instr. Am. hist, COL. NEW ROCHELLE, 69-72, ASST. PROF. AM. HIST. & DIR. AM. STUD, 72- George Washington Egleston Prize, Yale, 72. AHA; AAUP; Orgn. Am. Hist; Soc. Fr. Hist. Stud. Alexis de Tocqueville; European-American intellectual and cultural relations; American intellectual history. Publ: Contrib. Writing History, Appleton. 2nd ed. 67; auth, Alexis de Tocqueville describes the American character: two previously unpublished portraits. S.Atlantic Quart, (in press). Add: 220 Alston Ave, New Haven, CT 06515.

SCHLESINGER, ARTHUR, JR, b. Columbus, Ohio, Oct. 15, 17; m. 40; c. 4; m. 71; c. 1. AMERICAN HISTORY. A.B, Harvard, 38; Henry fel, Cambridge; Harvard Soc. fels; hon. L.H.D, Muhlenberg Col, 50, Tusculum Col, 66; hon. LL.D, Bethany Col, 56, New Sch. Social Res, 60; hon. D.C.L, Univ. N.B, 60. Assoc. prof. hist, Harvard, 46-54, prof, 54-61; spec. asst. to President of U.S, 61-64; ALBERT SCHWEITZER PROF. HUMANITIES, CITY UNIV. NEW YORK, 66- Pulitzer Prize Hist, 45, Biog, 65; Francis Parkman Prize, 57; Bancroft Prize, 58; Nat. Bk. Award, 65; Gold Medal, Nat. Inst. Arts & Lett, 67. U.S.A, 44-45. AHA; Orgn. Am. Hist. Publ: Age of Jackson, Little, 45; Age of Roosevelt, Vols. I-III, 57, 59 & 60, The politics of hope, 63, A thousand days: John F. Kennedy in the White House, 65. The bitter heritage, 67 & The crisis of confidence, 69, Houghton; ed, History of American Presidential elections & History of American political parties (4 vols), 73, Chelsea House. Add: Room 1606, 33 W. 42nd St, New York, NY 10036.

SCHLESINGER, BRUNO PAUL, b. Neunkirchen, Austria, Apr. 15, 11; U.S. citizen; m: c. 4. MODERN EUROPEAN HISTORY, POLITICAL THEORY. B.A, Univ. Vienna, 38; Ph.D, Univ. Notre Dame, 49. Vis. lectr. HIST. & POLIT. SCI ____ ____ARY'S COL.(IND), 45-46, instr, 46-49, asst. prof. 49-52, assoc. p____ ____ _____ CHMN. HUMANISTIC STUD, 68-, chmn. prog____ ____ ___ ____ ___ ____ grants, 57 & 60. AHA. His-t____ ____ ____ ____ Dawson and the : i-

Relig. Higher Educ. German e matic history, 1815-1914. Pub Waterloo, Appleton, 68. Add: '

SCHMIDT, ALBERT JOHN, b ____ ____ ____ ____ t____ ____ c. 3. ECONOMIC HISTORY. Pl ____ 36-38; Ph.D, Rutgers Univ, 46. ____p. 40-42, asst. prof, 46-51, assoc. p ____il____ rian, Europ. command, U.S. Dept ____.S., U.S. High Comnr. for Ger, 50-52 ____ C____ Hist. Asn; Agr. Hist. Soc; Orgn. ____ g l States; American social and cul' ____ Rural Hunterdon, an agricultura ____ e____ a three-hundred-year history, ____ x____ German foreign trade, 1949-19' ____ b Germany, 1949-1951, U.S. Dept Rutgers University, Newark, N

SCHMIDT, LESTER FREDERICH ____ c. 2. UNITED STATES INTEL 46. scholar. & A.M, 47; fel. & 55. Asst. sociol, Wayne State sci, Colo. State Col, 50-54, a: SOCIOL, BALL STATE UNIV, lectr, Rutgers Univ, 55-56; I 57; ed, Proc. Ind. Acad. Sc 45. AHA; Orgn. Am. Hist. A Clayton Ball, In: Dictionary Ball State University, Muncie

SCHMIDTLEIN, GENE F, b. S AMERICAN HISTORY 56; Ph.D, Univ M PHENS COL: States ''

Speech, Drama; Volume III, Foreign Languages, Linguistics, Philology; Volume IV, Philosophy, Religion, Law. Volume IV also includes a name index to all four volumes.

The *Directory of American Scholars* is devoted to scholars in the humanities, and is therefore a companion to *American Men and Women of Science*. It is compiled with the cooperation of the American Council of Learned Societies, a federation of twenty-eight national organizations whose memberships are all covered in the directory. University students can find no better quick source in which to check on the past accomplishments of their professors than the *Directory of American Scholars* and *American Men and Women of Science*. Note that the emphasis in both books is on scholars and teachers, not on professional practitioners; other biographical directories should be consulted for material on people who are practicing medicine, architecture, law, etc.

4. *Dictionary of American Biography*, edited under the auspices of the American Council of Learned Societies and published in 20 volumes between 1928 and 1936, with an index volume and five supplements, published up to 1977. A newer reprint edition contains the original 20 volumes plus the supplements. The *D.A.B.*, as librarians call it, contains no living subjects among its 16,000 biographees, all of whom were Americans.

Some *D.A.B.* articles have been superseded by more recent scholarship, the use of newly available documents and fresh interpretations. But with that taken into account, the *D.A.B.* remains a high quality reference work. Articles contain bibliographies. An abridgment of *D.A.B.*, published in 1954, is entitled the *Concise Dictionary of American Biography*. Researchers should not confuse this with the full version.

5. *Dictionary of National Biography*, the English counterpart and predecessor of the *D.A.B.* (above) is called the *D.N.B.* by librarians. The *D.N.B.* first appeared between 1885 and 1901 in 63 volumes (currently in 22 volumes), and has since been augmented by supplements every decade. It is published by the Oxford University Press. Like the *D.A.B.*, this massive work does not include biographies of living persons. It contains more than 32,000 biographies of people who lived in Britain and the British Commonwealth. There is also a *Concise Dictionary of National Biography*, in two volumes, published in 1952 (to 1900) and in 1961 (to 1950).

Reference Books That Open New Doors

See First:
The Best Guide to Reference Books (p. 24)
Finding Reference Books in Libraries (p. 25)
Know the Reference Book Catalogs (p. 49)

Some reference books have the special value of opening new doors for research, of suggesting new avenues, rather than simply providing the answers to specific questions. Here are a few door-openers among many:

1. *Free Out-of-Town Telephone Directories.* The business offices of many Bell System telephone companies make it a policy to supply out-of-town telephone directories on request and without charge to both home and business telephone subscribers. They do so because the limited number of subscribers who make numerous long distance calls will place calls more efficiently if they have the directories at hand. A researcher who needs to find names, addresses and telephone numbers in such major centers as New York, Washington, Chicago and Los Angeles can call the business office of his local company and order the books he needs. This service includes both street directories and classified (Yellow Pages). *Note:* organizations, trade associations and other groups that are sources of information are classfied in most Yellow Pages under "Associations."

2. *Polk's City Directories.* Many businessmen rely heavily on the more than 1,400 separate city directories compiled and published at regular intervals (in most cases annually) by R. L. Polk Co., 431 Howard Street, Detroit, Mich. 48231. City directories are more frequently found in large public (city) libraries than in university libraries. Based on data compiled by door-to-door canvass, or sometimes by telephone interview, city directories record the name of each resident over eighteen years of age, his address, marital status, occupation, place of employment, telephone number and whether his residence is owned or rented. Each business, professional or industrial firm in a directory canvass area is cataloged by type, and the owners, partners or corporate officers are listed. Polk directories cover many cities in the United States and Canada, and their suburbs. A notable exception is New York City, for which Polk has not published a directory since 1933. (Recently several other cities have grown too large for Polk to handle, so for a recent date you should check to see if there is a current directory.)

REPELLENTS: DOG
CAL: OAKLAND
Grant Laboratories 6020 Adeline .... A
CAL: SAN FRANCISCO
Chevron Chemical Co., Ortho Div. 200 Bush ...... AAAA
ILL: ROCK ISLAND
Nixalite Company of America 2509 Fifth Ave. (Birds,
Rodents & Animals) .... A
MASS: SUDBURY
Sudbury Laboratory, Inc. (Liquid & Powder, Also For
Cats, Rabbits & Mosquitoes) .... AA
MASS: WESTWOOD
Hammond Paint & Chemical Co. 107 Greenacre Rd.
(Dog & Crow) .... B
NY: GLENFORD
Nip-Co. Mfg., Inc. Rte. 28 (& Cat) .... AAA
NY: PLEASANT VALLEY
Nott Mfg. Co., Inc. (Also Deer, Rabbits, Mice) .... AAA

REPELLENTS: INSECT
CAL: BURLINGAME
NIECO DIV., NPI CORP. P.O. Drawer 4506 (Air
Screens) (415—697-7335) .... AAA
CAL: SAN FRANCISCO
Duart Mfg. Co., Ltd. 984 Folsom S
CONN: BRIDGEPORT
Acme United Corporation 100 Hic
DEL: WILMINGTON
Hercules Incorporated 917 King S
GA: ATLANTA
Zep Manufacturing Co. 3008 Olym
Blvd.
MASS: WOBURN
Blox Industries, Inc. 100 Ashburto
MINN: MINNEAPOLIS
McLaughlin Gormley King Co. 881U Tenth Ave. N.
(Bulk) .... AAAA
MO: ST. LOUIS
Huge Co. Inc. 884 Hodiamont Ave. .... AA
NJ: CAMDEN
Classic Chemical 16th & Mickle Sts. X
NJ: EDGEWATER
Octagon Process Inc. 12 Archer Ave. .... AAA
NY: FLUSHING
Termitrol Co. P.O. Box 825 .... AAA
NY: GLENFORD
Nip-Co. Mfg., Inc. Rte. 28 (General House/Garden
Chemicals) .... AAA
NY: NEW YORK
CHROMALLOY AMERICAN CORPORATION 641
Lexington Ave. (212—826-9277) .... AAAA
(See Our Corporate Insert in A-Z, Vol. 7, For Nearest
Sales Office of Division or Subsidiary.)
UNION CARBIDE CORP., HOME & AUTOMOTIVE
PRODUCTS DIV. 270 Park Ave. (212—551-
3763) .... AAAA
(See Union Carbide Corporate Insert in Vol. 7 for
Sales Offices & Products.)
NY: WATERVLIET
Lee, Wm. W., & Co., Inc. 1007 24 St. (Black Fl
Mosquitoes) ....
OHIO: CLEVELAND
State Chemical Mfg. Co. 3100 Hamilton Ave. .... AAAA
PA: PITTSBURGH
Mine Safety Appliances Company 408 Penn Center
Blvd. .... AAAA
TENN: MEMPHIS
Household Products Div. 701 N. Main St., P.O. Box
217 .... AAAA

REPELLENTS: MOSQUITO
**(see Insecticides: All Kinds, Liquid, Powder,
etc.)**

REPELLENTS: SHARK
PA: LANGHORNE
.... nts Inc. P.O. Box 157

REPELLENTS: STAIN & WATER
CAL: TORRANCE
Kenitex Chemicals Inc. 1234 Francisco ....
DEL: WILMINGTON
Du Pont, E. I., de Nemours & Co., Inc. 1007 Mark
(Textile & Soil) ....
GA: ATLANTA
AZS Chemical Co. 762 Marietta Blvd...............
ILL: CHICAGO
Keystone Aniline & Chemical Co. 321 N. Loomis
(Textile, Leather) ....
KY: LOUISVILLE
Ohio Falls, Inc. 733 E. Madison (Water).............
MASS: LEOMINSTER
Lukon Inc. 300 Whitney St. (& Grease) ....
MICH: ADRIAN
SWS Silicones Corp. Sutton Rd. (Silicone) ....
MO: NORTH KANSAS CITY
Golden Star Polish Mfg. Co., Inc. 400 E. 10th Ave

> **Thomas Register of American Manufacturers**
> is organized by products and furnishes
> a quick way of finding out what companies
> manufacture a given line of products.

Dixo Co., Inc. (Non-Aqueous Water Repellents) ....
NY: AMSTERDAM
Mohawk Finishing Products, Inc. Perth Rd...........
NY: BROOKLYN
Polymer Research Corp. of America 2186-87 Mi
Ave. (For Fabrics) ....
NY: TONAWANDA
Bisonite Co., Inc. 2248 Military Rd..................
NY: WATERFORD
GENERAL ELECTRIC CO., SILICONE PRODUCTS
DEPT. Section TR75 (Silicones For Textiles &
Masonry) (518—237-3330)..........................
    ♦ See our catalog in THOMCAT
NC: GUILFORD COLLEGE
Zimmerman Associates (Silicone) ....
PA: BRIDGEVILLE
Russell Standard Corp. 2 Prestley Rd.................
RI: LINCOLN
Hope Chemical Corp. Carrington St. ....
RI: PAWTUCKET
Dytex Chemical Co. 372 Central Ave. ....
Synthron, Inc. 44 East Ave. ....
RI: PROVIDENCE
Eastern Color & Chemical Co. 35 Livingston (Wa
Textile)..

REPLACERS: ELECTRIC LAMP
(see Hangers: Lamp)

REPLACERS: NON-DRY MILK
(see Food Products)

REPLACER: NON-FAT DRY MI
Provide — A special blend of strictly fresh whey
high quality soy flour replaces non fat dry milk
significant cost savings.

SWIFT EDIBLE OIL C

The first American city directory in book form was published for Boston in 1785. Since the mid-nineteenth century, well before telephone directories appeared, many American cities were covered by locally published city directories. R. L. Polk Co. was established in 1870 and grew into the dominant city directory publisher. Today small-town and county directories are published by the local newspaper.

3. *Thomas Register of American Manufacturers.* This is the best and handiest guide to finding out who manufactures what. The main part of *Thomas Register* is arranged according to product (such as clothespins, spark plugs, etc.), with the makers of each product listed geographically, and their size class indicated in rough terms. Other parts of this multi-volume annual carry alphabetical lists of manufacturers, of product trade names (such as Ivory Soap), of corporate divisions and subsidiaries, of boards of trade and chambers of commerce. Three volumes are made up of manufacturers' catalogs, organized and indexed. Thomas Publishing Company is at 461 Eighth Avenue, New York, N.Y. 10001.

4. *Gebbie House Magazine Directory.* Published at two-year intervals, this is a useful guide to company "house organs," the publications of a particular company, which may contain much material valuable in research even though they are frankly special-interest publications. Because company house organs are not indexed in the various indexes published by H. W. Wilson Co., and are usually not carried by libraries, the *Gebbie Directory* (which *is* in many libraries) is a valuable research aid. Organized by name of company, it tells almost everything about the company magazines that public relations firms, writers, photographers and artists would want to know. In some cases the editors will send individual copies on request, or add your name to the mailing list. *Gebbie Directory* is at P.O. Box 1111, Sioux City, Iowa 51102.

Note: House magazines published by individual companies should not be confused with the trade press, or business press, which consists of specialized business periodicals (mainly in magazine format, although some are in newspaper form) published for all who are interested in a given industry or economic activity. Many, but not all, trade press publishers are members of the American Business Press, Inc., 205 East 42nd Street, New York, N.Y. 10017. The contents of many trade publications are indexed in the appropriate indexes of H. W. Wilson Co. (see p. 49). Most of the trade or business periodicals are listed in *Standard Periodical*

Directory (see below) and in *Ulrich's International Periodicals Directory* (p. 91).

> *Now See:*
> *Search Out the Trade Press* (p. 89)

68,000 Periodicals Arranged by Subject

There are times in research when one wants to find out whether there are any periodicals devoted to a particular subject or interest, and if so, which are the most significant ones. This has been made much simpler since 1970 with the appearance of the *Standard Periodical Directory*, which is issued biennially by Oxbridge Communications, Inc., 183 Madison Avenue, New York, N.Y. 10016. This directory gives significant facts on more than 68,000 American and Canadian periodicals, grouped by 230 subject categories. Separate title and subject indexes assist the user in finding the periodical listing(s) he is seeking. Types of periodicals included are consumer magazines, trade journals, newsletters, government publications, house organs of companies, directories, proceedings of learned societies, yearbooks, and others. The *Standard Periodical Directory* thus makes it possible to identify periodicals which the researcher has never seen, and to find out a good deal about them, in subject fields in which he knows little or nothing. He can then try to obtain sample copies from the publisher or hunt them down in a special library.

Associations — Key to Finding Specialists

We are a nation of joiners. People with particular interests in common, whether they are hobbyists, professionals or businessmen, group together. They form clubs, professional societies, business organizations and trade associations through which to pursue their common interests in an organized way. They become acquainted with one another and learn what their fellow-members are doing. If a researcher wants to investigate a subject in which there are hundreds, even thousands, of specialists, it is highly useful to get in touch with the association of which they are likely to be members.

This is made easy by consulting the *Encyclopedia of Associations*, published by Gale Research Company (see p. 50), and brought up to date biennially. The encyclopedia is indexed in every possible way to be most useful — by broad subject categories, by very

1460 Music & Music Trades

ASCAP Jazz Notes
Lynn Farnol Group, Inc., 104 E. 78th St., New York, N.Y. 10021 (212) 988-3920
Ed. Dom Cerulli
1963 Q

ASCAP Today
American Society of Composers, Authors & Publishers, One Lincoln Plaza, New York, N.Y. 10023 (212) 595-3050
Ed. Walter Wager
Articles on ASCAP members and their achievements, plus current questions concerning composers, lyricists, music publishers.
1967 Q Free Circ 34,000 National 8 1/2 x 11 1/2 Letterpress 40pp.

ASUC Journal of Music Scores
Joseph Boonin, Inc., Box 2124, South Hackensack, NJ 07606
Ed. John Epperson
1973 3x/yr. $7.50 per copy Circ 175

Accent
Accent Publ. Co., 1418 Lake St., Evanston, IL 60204
Ed. Cliff Colnot, Bernie Dobroski
1976 5x/yr. $3 Circ 10,000 Adv

Accordion & Guitar World Magazine
607 Main St., Ridgefield, Conn. 06877
Ed. John C Gerstner
Aimed educationally at teachers, studio operators and professionals. Also some music trade dealers - helpful technical articles and special news items.
1936 M $3 $.50 per copy Circ 3,000 Adv

Adagio
A. Perrault, 1700 des Cascades St., Saint Hyacinthe, Que. J2S 3J1, Canada
Text: Eng. & Fr.
1975 BM

Agmazine
American Guild of Musical Artists, 1841 Broadway, New York, N.Y. 10023 (212) 265-3687
Ed. Sandra Munsell
1965 Q

Alberta Music Educator
University of Calgary, Dept. of Fine Arts, Calgary, Alta., Canada
Ed. Prof. E. Filipkowski
1965 3-4 times a year Circ 1,500

Allegro
Local 802 AFM, Associated Musicians of Greater New York, 261 W. 52 St., New Y N.Y. 10032 (212) 247-1200
Ed. Lester Salomon, Adv. Dir. Alex Smith
Music-labor information, technical articles about music, chess and other hobbies.
1921 11 times per year $3.30 $.30 per copy Back issues available per copy Circ 28,000 National Adv $500 11 1/2 x 16 Offset 24pp. Color

Amateur Chamber Music Players
15 W. 67th St., New York, N.Y. 10023
A directory giving the names, Addresses, telephone numbers and instruments played by members in the U.S.A. and 60 foreign countries.
1947 Irreg. Free Circ 6,000

Amateur Musician/Musicien Amateur
...

Articles concerning contemporary American music, featuring serious appraisals of contemporary composers with musical illustrations. 2000 words and more.
1952 Q Free Back issues available Circ 5,000

American Federation of Musicians Local 325
1717 Morena Blvd., San Diego, CA 92110
Ed. Vic Spies
M $3 Circ 2,500

American Fiddler News
American Old Time Fiddlers Assn., 6141 Morrill Avenue, Lincoln, Nebraska 68507 (402) 466-5519
Ed.-Publ. Delores DeRyke
Covers diverse fiddling styles — the traditional, old time, bluegrass, appalachian, ethnic, country/western, new generation. Also covers the fiddling-violinist, jazz violin, and blues.
1965 Q $5 $1.50 per copy Back issues available per copy Circ 6,000 International Adv $25 8 1/2 x 11 1/2 Mimeograph 40pp.

American Folk Music Occasional
Oak Publications, 33 W. 60th Street, New York, N.Y. 10023 (212) 246-0325
Ed. Chris Strachwitz
1970 Irreg. $2.95

American Guild of Authors and Composers, Bulletin
American Guild of Authors and Composers, 40 West 57th Street, New York, New York 10019 (212) 757-8833

American Guild of English Handbell Ringers Roster
American Guild of English Handbell Ringers, 1301 South Boston Ave., Tulsa, Okla. 74119
A

American Institute of Musicology, Miscellanea
P.O. Box 30665, Dallas, Texas 75230
Ed. Armen Carapetyan
1951 Irreg.

American Musical Digest
Gene Bruck, 245 W. 52nd St., New York

1948   ...per copy Circ 4,300 Adv
$120 4 ... d × . 1/2 Offset 160pp.

American Record Guide
A.R.G Publ., Inc., 1 Windsor Pl., Melville, NY 11746
Ed. Milton Caine
1977 M $7.50 Circ 41,300 Adv

American Recorder, The
American Recorder Society, Inc., 141 West 20th Street, New York, New York 10011 (212) 675-9042
Ed. Daniel R. Shapiro
Deals with the recorder and other early instruments for the amateur, school ...

specific subjects, by name of association, and geographically. Each entry includes such important facts as the purpose of the association, year of its foundation, size of membership, size of staff, publications, headquarters address, telephone, and name of executive. This makes it possible for a researcher not only to locate associations but also to distinguish the dominant and significant ones from the minor ones.

Among possible benefits of making contact with an association are: finding authorities to query (such as the association executive, officers and committee chairmen); reaching the association library, and possibly the librarian; finding the back files of the association's records; obtaining the association's publications, which may be virtually unknown to non-members; locating veteran members with long memories of past events; and finding members in your part of the country who can serve as your sources of information if the association headquarters is at an inconvenient distance. You probably could not find them so easily in any other way.

Government as an Information Source

Because federal government is concerned in some way with many of our activities and interests, it is a source of detailed information on a far greater scale than most laymen realize. The trick for the researcher in tapping government resources is to find what agency among hundreds in the executive branch, what person or persons within that agency, and what publications will be useful. In order to do this you should find out: (1) what executive branch agency, or agencies, have jurisdiction in your field of inquiry; and (2), what committees of the House and of the Senate have jurisdiction over legislation affecting those agencies. In some cases the path to the right agencies and committees is quite clear from their names. But in other cases there is no simple route, because your inquiry may lead to several agencies and several Congressional committees, each having a bearing on part of the subject.

When in doubt, you should first write to your Congressman for guidance to the right agencies and committees. A Congressional staff either knows or can find out fast. Further, to find the right executive branch agency the best single book is the *U.S. Government Organization Manual* (see p. 35), which is available in research libraries. It describes the origin and purpose of each government agency, and thus offers clear clues as to which ones to pursue for specialized information. Another step is to consult

774   **Section 8—HEALTH AND MEDICAL ORGANIZATIO'**

★8489★
AMERICAN INSTITUTE OF **NUTRITION** (AIN)
9650 Rockville Pike   Phone: (301) 530-7050
Bethesda, MD 20014   Dr. O. L. Kline, Exec. Officer
Founded: 1928. **Members:** 1600. Professional society of experimental nutrition
scientists from universities, government and industry. **Divisions:** Clinical
Nutrition (American Society for Clinical Nutrition, Inc.). **Publications:** (1)
American Journal of Clinical Nutrition, monthly; (2) Journal of Nutrition,
monthly. **Convention/ Meeting:** annual - always April. 1977 Chicago, IL; 1978
Atlantic City, NJ; 1979 Dallas, TX.

★8490★
AMERICAN SOCIETY FOR CLINICAL **NUTRITION** (ASCN)
9650 Rockville Pike   Phone: (301) 530-7050
Bethesda, MD 20014   A. L. Forbes, Sec.
Founded: 1960. **Members:** 350. Physicians and scientists actively engaged in
clinical nutritional research. To promote teaching, research, and reporting of
progress in human nutrition. **Publications:** The American Journal of Clinical
Nutrition, monthly. **Affiliated with:** American Institute of Nutrition (parent).
Convention/ Meeting: annual.

★8491★
ASSOCIATION OF STATE AND TERRIT(
   DIRECTORS
C/O Arizona Department Of Health Services
1740 W. Adams St.
Phoenix, AZ 85007
Founded: 1953. **Members:** 55. Directors of Public Health Nutrition Programs in
state or territorial health departments. **Convention/ Meeting:** irregular.

★8492★
COMMUNITY SYSTEMS FOUNDATION (**Nutrition**) (CSF)
2200 Fuller Rd.   Phone: (313) 761-1846
Ann Arbor, MI 48105   Frederick L. Goodman, Chm.
Founded: 1963. **Members:** 6. **Staff:** 4. Organization committed to the improvement
of mankind through the acquisition of knowledge which will lead to the
improvement of communities. Immediate focus is the understanding and
improvement of nutrition and its human consequences, since nutrition
throughout the world is a major and growing problem interrelating with many
aspects of the quality of life. Has conducted over 1100 health care studies.
Maintains library. **Publications:** Selected Abstract Listing, annual; also publishes
project reports. **Affiliated with:** CSF Australasia.

★8493★
FOOD AND **NUTRITION** BOARD (FNB)
2101 Constitution Ave., N.W.   Phone: (20.   .56
Washington, DC 20418   Paul E. Johnson, Exec.Sec.
Founded: 1940. **Members:** 15. **Staff:** 7. Evaluates nutritional science as it applies
to food processing and public health. Maintains library. Division of National
Academy of Science - National Research Council. **Committees:** Clinical Nutrition;
Dietary Allowances; Food Protection (Subcommittees: Food Microbiology;
Nonnutritive Sweeteners; Food Technology; Toxicology; Specifications - Food
Chemicals Codex); Food Science and Technology; GRAS List Survey - Phase III;
International Nutrition Programs (Subcommittees: Interactior '
Infections; Nutrition and Fertility); Nutrition; Brain Dev '
Nutrition and Dental Health; Nutrition of the Mot'

hospitals, colleges,
physicians, dentists,
Sponsors winter lectu
articles published du
Journal of Applied N
Personally (handbook
Nutrition. **Convention/**

★8496★
INTERNATIONAL !
C/O Prof. B. Isaks:
Institute Of Clinica
University Of Goth
Sahlgren's Hospita
S-41345 Gothenbur
Founded: 1946. **Mem**
recognized by the U
promote internation:
applications; to enc
                          of
                        by
                   othe
                   ecto
                  n/ N

_____)AT
489 Fifth Ave.
New York, NY 10017
Founded: 1941. **Membe**
and closely related ir
science of nutrition th
institutions, grants
monographs; fosters
provides objective, si
Maintains 2000- volun
and Nutrition Liaison
Knowledge in Nutriti
and educational mate

★8498★
NUTRITION TODAY SC
101 Ridgely Ave.
Annapolis, MD 2140∙
Founded: 1974. **Memb**
dentists, food techn∙
nurses, school food :
and concerned lay∙
knowledge. Seeks to
done for geography.
etc. Sponsors trave∙
Publications: Nutritior

> The **Encyclopedia of Associations**
> is the key to finding specialists
> in thousands of fields of particular
> study, hobby or occupation.

the card catalog of a research library for relevant government books and pamphlets that will indicate which agency was their point of origin.

As for Congressional committees, the *Congressional Directory* (see p. 35) lists committees of Congress, their members and the staff people who carry out committee work. In addition, the index to the *Congressional Record*, which is the daily report of sessions of Congress, shows which committees have reported certain bills to the House or Senate, or have had bills committed to them.

When the right executive branch agency is found, queries should be addressed to the Public Information Office of that agency. The PIO is financed and staffed to give information to the public, and its staff is usually very well informed and cooperative. You should always ask the PIO for citations of printed documents written by that agency (or others) and distributed by the Government Printing Office. Frequently inexpensive pamphlets are sent free as a quick answer to queries, whereas thicker pamphlets and books can be bought from the GPO, and sometimes from the agency. You can also inquire about material in the agency's specialized library (most have them), or in that of its parent department, which may be unavailable locally but which may be borrowed through Interlibrary Loan (see p. 96).

Although government people prefer to stick to public information channels, they can frequently put you in direct contact with an agency expert who may be the only person in all government with the specialized information that you seek. To get cooperation in reaching such experts it is best to go through the regular public information office channels.

In the case of Congressional committees, both House and Senate, queries should be sent to the clerk of the committee. Most useful materials that committees of Congress can supply you with are: bills (pending legislation) and public laws (legislation as enacted); committee reports on bills, which express the committee's opinion on why they should or should not be enacted; and hearings, which are books of printed testimony offered at public committee hearings while a bill is under consideration. Printed committee hearings on a given subject often represent an exhaustive study, and may provide the most scholarly, all-embracing set of documents extant. For a certain time after they are published, hearings are distributed free by the committee of origin and by members of Congress. Later they must be bought from the GPO.

With the recent development of *microform* (reduced size) publishing (see p. 114) it has become easier and cheaper for libraries to acquire and store Congressional committee hearings and reports, as well as the *Congressional Record*. For instance, Readex Microprint Corporation (101 5th Avenue, New York, N.Y. 10003) reproduces these Congressional materials on 6″ × 9″ *microprint* cards, each card containing 100 pages of print. Another publisher, Congressional Information Service, Inc. (7101 Wisconsin Avenue, Washington, D.C. 20014), has reproduced rare Congressional hearings of the past, extending back to 1839, on *microfiche* (see p. 114). Libraries that lack these Congressional research materials now may acquire them soon in some miniature form.

> *Now See:*
> *Government Printing Office* (below)
> *Your Congressman Can Help* (p. 68)
> *Using the Congressional Record* (p. 70)
> *The National Archives* (p. 109)

Government Printing Office

> *See First:*
> *Government as an Information Source* (p. 62)

As the publication house for the federal government, the Government Printing Office in Washington, D.C., produces a great variety of printed matter valuable to serious researchers. More than 24,000 GPO titles are available from the Superintendent of Documents. Subject matter ranges over every field in which an agency of federal government takes an interest. The agencies write and edit them; the GPO prints them and distributes them through the Superintendent of Documents.

Unfortunately, GPO publications are insufficiently known to the public because: (1) most book retailers don't stock them; (2) the GPO does almost no advertising; and (3) it maintains only 25 bookstores in the entire country. Most of them, including the one in the GPO building in Washington, D.C., stock only 1,500 to 2,000 different titles, so a buyer cannot always examine a GPO publication before putting out his cash. However, ordering in person from a GPO outlet in the Washington area gets quick results, often within a day or two, because the GPO keeps a full line in its warehouse in nearby Laurel, Maryland.

The other 24 GPO outlets are in five federal government departments in Washington, D.C., and in Atlanta, Birmingham, Boston, Chicago, Cleveland, Columbus, Dallas, Denver, Detroit, Houston,

ENVIRONMENT

72T9 ACTION HANDBOOK: MANAGING GROWTH IN THE SMALL COMMUNITY. A set of three handbooks presenting a process for community management. *Part I, Getting a Picture of What's Ahead,* provides an overview of the community management process and is of special interest to those who would initiate community management action. *Part II, Getting the Community Involved and Organized,* outlines approaches to community organization and involvement and suggests a working model for community organizers. *Part III, Community Action and Growth Management,* will be of special interest to those closely involved in making government work to manage growth. Three volumes, sold only as a set. 1978. 3 vols, 280 p. il.
EP 1.8:Ac 8/pt 1–3
S/N 055–000–00172–3   **$5.25**

73T9 GUIDELINES FOR IMPROVING THE MOBILE HOME LIVING ENVIRONMENT: INDIVIDUAL SITES, MOBILE HOME PARKS & SUBDIVISIONS There are 5.3 [...]
US. The [...]
the livab [...]
or subd [...]
study a [...]
setting, [...]
action [...]
mobile [...]
many pl [...]
p. il.
HH 1.6/ [...]
S/N 02: [...]

74T9 TORNADO PREPAREDNESS PLANNING. See page 14.
C 55.102:T 63/2/1978
S/N 003–017–00434–1   **$1.40**

77T9 WORLD POPULATION 1977: RECENT DEMOGRAPHIC ESTIMATES FOR THE COUNTRIES AND REGIONS OF THE WORLD. Presents comprehensive, annotated demographic data for all the countries and territories of the world. 1978. 449 p. il.
C 3.205/3:WP-77
S/N 003–024–01583–8   **$6.25**

78T9 MANAGEMENT OF WINTERING BALD EAGLES. Covered topics include food supply, habitat, species characteristics and range, winter behavior, human disturbance, and more. Contains many photographs and drawings. 1978. 59 p. il.
I 49.2:Ea 3/5
S/N 024–010–00490–8   **$2.40**

79T9 THE GREAT SALT LAKE. The Great Salt Lake, located in the desert area of western Utah, is unique because of its size and salt content. This booklet recounts the history and economic benefits of the lake and discusses the life forms in and around the lake. Filled with color photographs, maps, and drawings. 1978. 16 p. il.
I 19.2:G 79/2
S/N 024–001–03132–9   **$1.10**

80T9 COASTAL MAPPING HANDBOOK. The *Handbook* provides guidance in determing coastal mapping requirements. Sections on sources of assistance and advice and product and data sources are included. The many color maps and photographs and an extensive glossary of mapping terms are especially helpful. 1978. 199 [...]
5/3:C 63
024–001–03046–2   **$5.25**

[...]NCE AND TECHNOLOGY

81T9 OMNIDATA: AN INTERAC[...] SYSTEM FOR DATA RETRIEV[...]

Selected U.S. Government Publications, sent free eleven times a year to anyone who requests it, describes about 150 popular publications in each issue.

Jacksonville, Kansas City, Los Angeles, Milwaukee, New York, Philadelphia, Pueblo, San Francisco and Seattle.

The researcher must therefore make special effort to find out whether there are government publications in print that would be useful to him. If they are not to be found in a local library, and if he is not within reach of a GPO outlet, he must order them from the GPO by mail. This is especially the case with pamphlets, which most libraries do not collect. Orders with the correct title or stock number, and correct price, should be addressed to: Superintendent of Documents, U.S. Government Printing Office, Washington, D.C. 20402. Telephone inquiries: (202) 783-3238.

One way to start is to check a research library to see if it carries either the *Monthly Catalog of U.S. Government Publications*, which contains between 1,200 and 2,200 titles in each issue, or the shorter monthly *Selected List of U.S. Government Publications*. The *Monthly Catalog* is widely available in libraries, and subscriptions to it cost more than the average person would normally wish to pay ($55 a year). The typical monthly issue contains about 250 new titles or new versions of older publications. *Selected List of U.S. Government Publications*, on the other hand, is a 16-page booklet designed for individual use, and describes about 150 popular publications in each issue. It is distributed free eleven times a year to anyone who writes to the Superintendent of Documents and requests it. By examining this selected list regularly, you can get a good idea of the range of subject matter and the prices of government publications, particularly instructional and descriptive booklets which the GPO considers of most general public interest.

Another way to start is to write to the GPO or to your Congressman for a copy of the free 8-page brochure entitled *Subject Bibliography Index*. This brochure contains a list of 270 subject bibliographies (formerly called "price lists") of GPO publications. Each subject bibliography describes the printed material that GPO offers in one subject area, such as: Consumer Information, Fish and Marine Life, National Parks, and Solar Energy. Mark the subject bibliographies in which you are interested and mail the marked page to the Superintendent of Documents. You should receive the subject bibliographies you ordered within two or three weeks.

The subject bibliographies are pamphlets that give the basic information on each of the GPO books, booklets, charts, maps and leaflets in the given subject area. For instance, you can find that *Edible and Hazardous Marine Life*, an Air Force survival booklet, has 38 pages, contains dozens of color illustrations, was revised in

1978 and costs $1.90. With this information and the booklet serial number you can order the individual titles you want from the GPO by mail. The GPO accepts checks. VISA and Master Charge cards are accepted at GPO bookstores.

From such information in the free bibliographies you can decide whether to buy inexpensive publications by mail before seeing them. In the case of bound books, which cost more, you may be able to examine them at one of the GPO retail stores in the cities listed above. Or you may find them in a local library.

Another way to avoid making a blind purchase is to call the Federal Building in your city to see if by chance someone in a branch office of the government agency concerned with the publication (such as the Department of Labor, or Agriculture) will permit you to examine his desk copy. Or if one of the General Services Administration Federal Information Centers is in your city (consult telephone directory under *U.S. Government*) see if you can get help there. If not, you may have to decide to buy the book without examining it first.

Now See:
   Your Congressman Can Help (below)

Your Congressman Can Help

See First:
   Congressional Directory (p. 35)
   Government Printing Office (p. 65)
   Government as an Information Source (p. 62)

Because they have quick access to the Library of Congress, the Government Printing Office (GPO), the committees of Congress and the executive agencies of government, your representatives in Congress can help you in research in several ways. They are happy to assist any resident of their district who writes a letter requesting a reasonable service, on the theory that by serving voters they make and keep friends. Every Congressional office has employees doing what is called on Capitol Hill "case work" — helping constituents deal with Washington bureaucracy.

In all but the most sparsely populated states, it is better to ask help from your Representative, rather than from a Senator, because the former has fewer constituents to serve. But the efficiency of service depends finally on the quality and attitude of the employee who processes your request. You may get efficient, thoughtful service from a staff member who reads your letter with care and understands exactly what you want. On the other hand, the writer has seen a number of cases where staff people both in Congressional offices and in executive agencies of government have clearly given no real attention to the question asked, and have carelessly mailed back printed matter that is only distantly related to the subject-matter of the inquiry. Usually, however, a follow-up letter calling attention to the non-response is given the proper treatment and obtains good results. One must have patience.

When writing to your Representative, state at the outset that you are a constituent and give your home address. Put your request in the most concise possible form so that it can be understood and acted on promptly. Your letter is one among hundreds; it will be acted on at once if the case worker can see at a glance what needs to be done to serve you. Whenever possible, ask for printed matter that will answer your question; do not ask so many questions that the office must compose a detailed letter, which takes time to dictate and transcribe.

Mailing is free of charge to Members of Congress, and a certain amount of GPO literature is available to them for free distribution, particularly small pamphlets. Most Congressional documents are also free — but not the bound *Congressional Directory.*

Some services that a Congressional office can provide are:

1. A call to the Government Printing Office for a list of publications in a specified field, from which you can select and order direct from the GPO.

2. A call to the Public Information Officer of a federal government agency to find its latest publications in your field of inquiry.

3. Copies of House and Senate bills, committee hearings (testimony) and committee reports.

4. Information on the status of pending legislation.

5. Local information — on sights, historic shrines, national parks, and so forth in their own districts. For this, write to the Representative whose district is concerned, not to your own Representative.

In addition, Members of Congress can transmit to the Library of Congress, through the Congressional Research Service (CRS) of the Library, requests from their constituents for information that can be answered easily. An official CRS pamphlet addressed to Members of Congress expresses its policy this way:

"Constituents

"While we cannot undertake research for your constituents — please, no term papers or master's theses! — we do try to help with that portion of your constituent mail which can be answered with readily available material. Rather than telephoning such inquiries, many congressional offices find it faster and more convenient to send the letters directly to CRS; however, it is important to forward them in a timely manner. The Service will return them with the appropriate materials for transmittal to constituents."

In short, the CRS will try to answer reasonable queries as a service to Members of Congress. No one should take undue advantage of this service, but it is nice to know it is there.

> *Now See:*
> *Using the Congressional Record* (below)

Using the Congressional Record

> *See First:*
> *Government as an Information Source* (p. 62)
> *Your Congressman Can Help* (p. 68)

The *Congressional Record*, printed daily when Congress is in session, is a highly useful source of information on matters of current interest as well as a gold mine for historians and biographers. The main body of the *Congressional Record* is a verbatim transcript (sometimes edited) of the words spoken on the floor of the U.S. Senate and the House of Representatives. In addition, the Appendix to the record includes all kinds of papers which Members of Congress arrange to have inserted into the record as "extensions" of their remarks, without reading them aloud. These include speeches given by Members outside the Congressional chambers, newspaper editorials and the like. Page sequence runs in three groups: S-number pages are the Senate record; H-number pages are the House record; and E-number pages are for Extension of Remarks, though in past years they were designated A for Appendix.

What makes the *Congressional Record* so valuable in research is its index, which is compiled fortnightly during the annual sessions of Congress, and is cumulated after the session adjourns into one alphabetical index for the session. The index covers items in both floor action and the Extension of Remarks, and is meticulously maintained by name and subject.

This makes it possible for you to find quickly the page references to every speech or passing remark made by any Member of Congress, every paper he introduced into the *Record,* and every bill he sponsored. Under a given subject (such as "narcotics" or "income taxes") you can find who discussed it on the floor; what bills concerning it were introduced, or acted on by either house or by committees; and what articles and speeches touching on it were

---

CONGRESSIONAL RECORD INDEX

Kennedy, Edward M.

Appendices
Development of the Tax Expenditure Concept, S17482
Sunset Legislation and Tax Expenditures—Technical Implementation, S17483
Appointments
Conferee on S. 1487, cigarette bootlegging bill, S17901
Conferee on S. 1613, Magistrates Act of 1978, S17637
Conferee on S. 2416, nurse training amendments, S17900
Conferee on S. 2466, Health Services Research, Health Statistics, and Health Care Technology Act, S17899
Conferee on S. 2474, Health Services Extension and Primary Health Care Act, S18846
Conferee on S. 2534, Health Maintenance Organization Amendments, S17895
Conferee on S. 2570, CETA amendments, S16884
Conferee on S. 3151, Dept. of Justice appropriations, S16891
Articles and editorials
Bricking up an Antitrust Loophole, New York Times, S17979
Congress Should Act To Uphold Lawsuits, Tallahassee (Fla.) Democrat, S17980
Dangers in Lebanon (sundry), S19427, S19428
Floods Ravage Southeast—Vietnam and Laos Appeal for Aid, Washington Post, S17881 •
Indirect Purchasers Bill Facing a Probable Death, Carole Shifrin, Washington Post, S17981
Labs and the Test Ban, Washington Post, S19491 •
Let Overcharge Victims Sue, Salt Lake City (Utah) Deseret News, S17978
Money Is There for the Capital Spending, Business Week, S17952
Nix the Fixers, St. Petersburg (Fla.) Times, S17980
Oregon Official Pushing for Federal Price-Fixing Legislation, Portland (Oreg.) Oregonian, S17981
Price Fixing, Columbus (Ohio) Citizen-Journal, S17978
Pursuing the Price Fixers, W...

Human rights: Nicaraguan violations, S17397 •
Humphrey, Senator Muriel: tribute, S19648 •
Immigration and Nationality Act: retention of U.S. citizenship of children born overseas (H.R. 13349), S16875 •
Income taxes: reduction (H.R. 13511), S17188, 7329, 7386, 7484, 7562–7671, 7778, 7951, 7976, 130 •, 509), If of Tax

> **The Congressional Record Index** indicates the speeches and actions of all members of Congress, and gives the pages in the **Congressional Record** where details are printed. (See illustration of CONGRESSIONAL RECORD, next page.)

Massachusetts: Federal judgeship situation, S1751
Medicare-Medicaid Administrative and Reimbursement Reform Act: enact (H.R. 5285), S18355, S18358, S18359, S18361, S18362, S18382, S18384, S18385, S18390–S18394, S18397, S18398, S18400–S18403, S18407, S18408
National health insurance: outline of proposed program, S16813–S16817
National Parks and Recreation Act: authorizing appropriations (S. 791), S18532 •
Natural gas: conference report on National Energy Policy Act (H.R. 5289), S17007 •
Nicaragua: human rights violations, S17397 •
———suspension of assistance to, S19492 •
Nuclear weapons: comprehensive test ban, S19491 •
Oil Pollution Liability, and Compensation Act: (S. 1701) •

CONGRESSIONAL RECORD — SENATE   S 16813

respect to any resolution still pending before a committee on September 1, of the second session of a Congress, the committee shall be automatically discharged and the resolution placed on the appropriate calendar.

"(d) The provisions of section 912 of title 5, United States Code, relating to t~ eration of r~

(See Congressional Record Index, on previous page.)

suspend momen-
advised that the
ts were set aside
amendment of the
would be out of or-
ttee amendments are

. President, I suggest
uorum.
Mr. President, who has

PRESIDENT pro te~
r from Maine has the

Mr. President, the com-
t which is involved is
ecommended by the
vironment and Pub-
gh there is no time
erstood that the staffs
son, interested Sen-
mittee on Enviro~
Works, and Senator
orking over the week-
ernative to the com-
That work is under-
ideration, and the
ing the amendment
give us time to work
ient.
liamentary inquiry?
nderstanding of all
the leadership, that
e of putting it over,
e understanding on
that we would pro-
ment the first thing
ough it was not the
mous-consent request.
n view of the fact that
ctly involved are not
or at this time I sug-
f a quorum.
PRESIDENT pro te~
ill call the roll.
legislative clerk pro-
oll.
. President, I ask.

unanimous consent that the order for the quorum call be rescinded.

Mr. LONG. I object.

The ACTING PRESIDENT pro te~ pore. Objection is heard.

The assistant legi~

Mr. KENNEDY. Mr. President, I ask unanimous consent that the order for the quorum call be rescinded.

The PRESIDING OFFICER. Without objection, it is so ordered.

NEW NATIONAL HEALTH INSUR-ANCE PROGRAM

Mr. KENNEDY. Mr. President, today I am pleased to make public an outline of a significant new national health insur-ance program, prepared by the Com-mittee for National Health Insurance in collaboration with my office.

It is nearly 10 years since CNHI was formed. Its goal was and is to achieve high quality health care for all Ameri-cans as a matter of right, within a sys-tem that brings runaway health costs under control.

Many aspects of American life have changed since CNHI was formed in 1968. Many of these changes have been posi-tive and have enriched the quality of life for millions of Americans. But in one area—the health area—the crisis which was just emerging in 1968 has grown se-riously worse. The major reason has been the runaway escalation of health care costs.

This rampant inflation takes its toll everywhere—on Federal budgets where the percentage of the Federal dollar spent on health has risen from 4.3 per-cent in 1963 to 12.7 percent this year; on State budgets where Medicaid costs have become the single most rapidly es-calating cost; on corporations which pay more and more each year for health benefits; on the American family which must pay $2,115 today, and $3,590 in 1983 for benefits which cost $533 in 1963; on the elderly, who pay more for their care today out of their own pocket than the year Medicare was implemented.

Hospital costs are so out of control that usually rational people talk about inserted into the *Record* in the Extension of Remarks. Given the range of interest of Congress and its 535 Members, the index to the *Congressional Record* is therefore one of great scope and of fine detail.

Many reference libraries carry the bound volumes of the *Congressional Record* and its index, which are published a few months after the final adjournment of each session. There is no cumulation of the index embracing more than one session, which is approximately one year. Volumes are numbered by the number of the Congress, with each part specifically identifying by month and year the period its contents cover. (The First Congress met in 1789; the 96th Congress was elected in 1978.)

When it is inconvenient to consult current issues in your local library, you can subscribe to the *Congressional Record* (bound sets, or daily by mail) or buy individual copies for a modest price through the Government Printing Office. Sometimes Congressmen supply a few designated recent back issues as a courtesy.

Using the Library of Congress

See First:
Government as an Information Source (p. 62)
Your Congressman Can Help (p. 68)

No matter where you are, you can use the Library of Congress, the biggest library in the country, and you need not make a trip to Washington to do it. Although in form this collection is what its name suggests, namely, a resource created by Congress for its own use, the Library of Congress by historical evolution has grown into the national library of the United States. In effect, it is open to all and serves anyone above high school age who wants to use it.

The greatest asset of the LC, as one might expect, is its huge collection of more than 18,000,000 books and pamphlets. It also holds millions of other items, such as newspapers, periodicals, manuscripts, maps, sheet music, photographs, phonograph records, prints, drawings, motion picture reels, microfilm reels and posters. More than 7,000 items of all kinds are added to the collections daily. To use the LC collections other than bound books, a trip to the Library is necessary.

The LC card catalog can be a help to anyone preparing a bibliography for a serious research project. There is a common misconception that "the Library of Congress keeps a copy of every book published in the U.S." This is not true, because the LC is selective in acquiring books. But the size and breadth of its holdings of both old and recently published books and pamphlets must be seen to be believed. Of particular value is the inclusion of Congressional committee reports and studies, which the LC binds and catalogs as books even though many are pamphlet size, and these are not often found in most reference libraries.

The most effective and satisfying way to find out what the Library can do for you is to consult the card catalog yourself. *Warning:* at the start, be sure not to confuse the catalog in the Main Reading Room (main floor, Main Building) with the card catalog on the fifth floor of the Thomas Jefferson Building, formerly called the Library Annex. The former is the larger, more comprehensive catalog. It has grown from the opening of the Library's Main Building in 1897, whereas the card catalog in the Thomas Jefferson Building dates from 1939 when it was opened. Cards for many of the older books antedating 1939 are not included there, and cards printed since 1969 are no longer filed there. Furthermore, the task of filing new cards and catching up on filing old ones is so great that the work does not always progress on schedule, with the result that title and subject cards for a given book may be missing from the card catalog long after the author card has been filed. It is therefore good practice to search author, title and subject before concluding that the Library of Congress does not have a certain book.

If you cannot visit the Library of Congress, there are several other ways to proceed. One is to write to your Congressman (see p. 68) and ask him to have his staff put your research request to the Library. The LC Congressional Research Service answers some Congressional research queries on behalf of constituents (see p. 70 for LC policy on this), and the Congressman's office can then send the results to you.

Another method of consulting the LC card catalog from a distance is to have your own personal friend or agent, someone who knows library research methods, to consult the catalog for you. The LC General Reading Rooms Division maintains a list of people who will do reference work for a fee.

Still another method, and a far from satisfactory one although graduates of library science schools dutifully recommend it, is to consult the printed, bound volumes in your local reference library in which LC catalog cards are printed in reduced size, three columns to a page. Do not confuse these with the National Union Catalog volumes, which look like them and are usually shelved close by (see p. 94). The Library of Congress catalog volumes have been published in several alphabetical series, one every few years since 1942. Their contents have *NOT* been cumulated in one alphabetical series. There are separate series for author and subject cards. You must therefore be certain to consult all the available series (they total hundreds of volumes) before giving up. If you know the year of publication, start with the volume covering that date. You may be lucky and find the reproduced card for which you are searching quickly. Or you may find book references in the subject index which you want to add to your bibliography. But if you do not find what you want, do not conclude there is no entry for that book in the Library of Congress card catalog. You should then employ one of the other research methods described above.

The General Reading Rooms Division of the Library of Congress (Washington, D.C. 20540) answers written queries on reference matters, provided letters of inquiry make it clear that the researcher has first used the local and regional resources and still needs help. Because time and manpower are short, the LC has to limit the reference queries it can undertake to answer, so researchers should make clear that they have done a thorough job close to home, and should detail the bases they have covered.

Now See:
Using the National Union Catalog (p. 94)
Interlibrary Loan (p. 96)
Buying Library of Congress Catalog Cards (p. 98)
The National Archives (p. 109)

Information Networks at Your Service

In research, it is often productive to pause and ask yourself: Who can help me? What people, what organizations, have material that I need?

Your answer to this kind of thinking about your methods of research may lead you down highly rewarding paths to new sources of information. I call these paths "information networks." Here are seven of them:

1. DAILY AND WEEKLY NEWSPAPERS. Consult the *Editor & Publisher International Yearbook*, which is in many reference libraries and newspaper offices. It is produced by the weekly trade journal of the newspaper industry, *Editor & Publisher*. The *E&P Yearbook* is arranged geographically. It lists the daily and weekly newspapers of the United States and Canada, and carries a detailed listing of the officers and editors of each newspaper. From it you

I-54—Florida

LAKELAND, FLA.
Polk County

'70 U.S. Census—41,550; '79 Est. 55,884
ABC-CZ (70): 76,510 (HH 25,243)
ABC-CZ (78): 92,900 (HH 34,100)

THE LEDGER (eS)

Lakeland Ledger Publishing Corp., PO Box 408,
Lakeland, FL 33802; tel (813) 687-7000;
New York Times group.
Note: Paper changed April 30, 1979, to morning
from evening publication.
Circulation: 37,635 (e-mon to fri); 37,635 (e-
sat); 43,440 (S); ABC Circulation average for
12 months ended Sept. 30, 1978.
Price: 15¢(d); 15¢(sat); 35¢(S); $4.55/mo.
Advertising: Open line rate 53¢(m); 53¢(e);
53¢(S). **Representative:** Branham/News-
papers Sales.
News services: AP; NYT. **Politics:** Independent.
Established: 1924.
Supplement: Family Weekly (S).

CORPORATE OFFICERS
President   John Harrison
Vice Pres   Elven Grubbs
Secy   Michael Ryan
Treas   Ralph Bowman
Controller   Reginald Davenport

GEN'L MGMT. & BUSINESS
Publisher   Elven Grubbs
Controller   Howard Staik
ADVERTISING DEPARTMENT
Adv Mgr   John Gilman
Ret Adv Mgr   Don Whitworth
Class Adv Mgr   Fred Trubey
Class Sales Mgr   Linda Bronson
CIRCULATION DEPARTMENT
Circ Dir   James Johnson
NEWS EXECUTIVES
Editor   Louis M. Perez
Man Editor   Tim J. McGuire
City Editor   Will Corbin
Asst City Editor   Keith Moyer

EDITORS & MANAGERS
Action Line   Bobbie Rossiter
Amusements   Susan Barbosa
Books   Lynne Croft
Business   Clint Duke
Editor of Ed Page Louis M. Perez
Education   Nancy Stohs
Fashion   Lynne Croft
Garden   Lynne Croft
Food   Jane Nickerson
Home Furnishings   Lynne Croft
Life Style   Lynne Croft
Music   Susan Barbosa
Outdoor   Richard Lemanski
Photo Dept Mgr   Rudolph Faircloth
Television-Radio   Bobbie Rossiter
Travel   Lamar Thames

MECHANICAL DEPARTMENT
Prod Dir   Robert Douglass
Comp Room Foreman Wayne Looney
Engraving Foreman James Fuller
Stereo Foreman   Bruce Erbeck
Market information: Zoned editions; split run;
total market coverage; ADS—The Ledger "E".
Mechanical available: Offset; black and 3 ROP
colors; inserts accepted—preprinted, hi-fi,
spectacolor.
Mechanical specifications: Type page 1...

News service: AP. **Politics:** Independent.
Established: 1876.
Not Published: Christmas.
Special Editions: Progress (Jan.); Fun & Art (Spr-
ing) Cookbook (Fall); Back-to-School (Aug.);
Homes (Oct.); Christmas Gift Guide (Nov.).
Special Pages: Food Pages every Wed. and Sun-
day; Church Friday.
Magazines: Family Weekly (Sun.); Own. TV Today
(Sun.), offset.

GEN'L MGMT. & BUSINESS
Publisher   James M. Brown
Controllers   Walt Garris, Dan Friedman

ADVERTISING DEPARTMENT
Adv Mgr   Ken Pass
Class Adv Mgr   David Elbert
CIRCULATION DEPARTMENT
Circ Mgr   Bob Gulick
NEWS EXECUTIVES, EDITORS & MANAGERS
Editor   Allan Smith
Executive Editor   Marie Bolles
News Editor   Marjorie North
Newsfeatures Editor Deanne Brandon
Sports Editor   Stan McNeal
Medicine   Dave Weber

MECHANICAL DEPARTMENT
Prod [...]
Printi[...]
Marke[...]
total [...]
Mech[...]
color[...]
spect[...]
Mech[...]
21 1/[...]
Comr[...]
133,7[...]
56,41[...]
Equip[...]
1100 [...]
PROD[...]
1-CO[...]
LE.[...]
PRESSROOM: 6-G/Suburbanite (1 folders).
MAILROOM: Bundle tyers—1-St.

MARIANNA, FLA.
Jackson County

'70 U.S. Census—6,741; '79 Est. 7,626
City Zone—6,600 (HH 2,186)

JACKSON COUNTY FLORIDAN (e-tues to fri; S)

Jackson County Floridan, 104 E Lafayette St.
Marianna, FL 32446.
Circulation: 4,906 (e-tue to fri); 5,269 (S);
Sworn Sept 30, 1978.
Price: 15¢(d); 25¢(S); $3.25/mo.
Advertising: Open line rate 17¢(e); 17¢(S).
News service: AP. **Politics:** Independent.
Established: 1956.

GEN'L MGMT. & BUSINESS
Publisher and Genl Mgr   Harold Odom
ADVERTISING DEPARTMENT
[...] Swanson

DIARIO LAS AMERICAS (m-tues to sat; S) (Spa...)

Diario Las Americas, 2900 NW 39th S[...]
FL 33142; tel (305) 633-3341.
Circulation: 54,428 (m-tue to fri); 54[...]
sat); 54,428 (S); Sworn Sept 30, 1978.
Price: 20¢(d); 20¢(sat); 35¢(S); $3.75/[...]
yr.
Advertising: Open line rate 65¢(m); 65¢[...]
News services: UPI; Agence France[...]
Politics: Independent. **Established:** 1[...]
Not Published: Day after New Years D[...]
Friday; Memorial Day; Fourth of Ju[...]
Day; Thanksgiving; Christmas.
Special Editions for 1979: Youth Fair[...]
Brides (April), Cuban Independe[...]
(May 20), Summer Fashions (June[...]
Furnishings (July), Back to School ([...]
Latin Chamber of Commerce (Au[...]
Cars of '80 (Oct. 27), Christmas [...]
Guide (Dec. 8)

GEN'L MGMT. & BUSINESS
Publisher   Horaci[...]
Business Manager   Victor[...]
Controller   Victor[...]
Credit Mgr   Jose[...]

ADVERTISING DEPARTMENT
                   Enrique[...]
[...]sor   Migu[...]
                   Enrique[...]
                   Maria[...]

[...]EPARTMENT
                   Guillermo[...]

[...]VES   Horac[...]
                   Guillermo[...]

[...]NAGERS
                   Carmencita S[...]
                   Guillermo[...]
                   C[...]
                   Ignacio[...]

Market information: Zoned editions;
total market coverage; ADS—Di[...]
Americas "A".
Mechanical available: Offset; black an[...]
colors; inserts accepted—preprint[...]
spectacolor, Free-Fall, Cards, etc.[...]
Mechanical specifications: Type page [...]
21"; E—8 cols, 10 picas, 12 points betw[...]
8 cols, 10 picas, 12 points between; C—[...]
picas, 18 points between.
Equipment: EDITORIAL: Perforator[...]
4961A; 7200 2-COM/SM. CLASSI[...]
electronic cps—1-HI/CTY (4 VDTs).[...]
Layout—Comp IV 2-COM/88.[...]
PRODUCTION: Typesetters—2-COM/[...]
1-COM/4967 TL, 3-COM/2961 HS;[...]
posers—1-N/FT40LNS; plate processo[...]
28; cameras—1-C/1244, 1-ITEK/440;[...]
film processors—1-LE/LD-24; shrink [...]
Standard SQU-7/335.
PRESSROOM: 7-G/U-686 (1 folder[...]
ROOM: Bundle tyers—1-ID, 1-Bu/1[...]
sers—1-KR.

THE MIAMI HERALD (m[...]

The Miami Herald Publishing Co., He[...]
Miami, FL 33101; tel (305) 3[...]
Knight-Ridder Newspapers group.
Note: The Miami HERALD and Miami [...]
corporately and editorially separa[...]
a contract The Miami Herald Pub[...]
is agent for all busines[...]
tion.[...]

can find the names of newspaper reporters and editors in every city and significant town, with the specialties of each in subjects as diverse as sports, crime, business, theater, food, art and politics.

Further, newspapers frequently keep clipping files in their libraries, organized by name and subject. The newspaper librarian will often fill a request for background material on a specific subject — especially if it can be easily duplicated from clippings by Xerox or a similar process. Thus the *E&P Yearbook* leads you quickly to the local newspaper experts on many topics in all parts of the country, and to what they have written.

2. PUBLIC RELATIONS SOURCES. See *Public Relations Sources* (p. 42). An excellent guide to useful information of many kinds produced by public relations sources is the popular paperback book, *1001 Valuable Things You Can Get Free*, by Mort Weisinger (Bantam). Names and addresses of information sources are kept up to date in new editions every two years.

3. CONGRESSIONAL OFFICES. See *Your Congressman Can Help* (p. 68). Remember that your own Congressman, or Senator, is most helpful in finding out facts for you from agencies of federal government. But for information on another part of the country than your home you should consult the Congressman or Senator who represents that area. A Member of Congress, with his staff, keeps voter lists, local telephone directories, city directories and newspapers published in the district he represents, so he knows people, places and events intimately.

The quickest way to find your Congressman's name is by consulting the *Congressional Directory*. In this book the boundaries of all Congressional districts are described and biographical matter is given on each Member of Congress. There are Congressional district maps in the back pages, but these maps fail to delineate clearly the boundary lines of Congressional districts in big cities. If you do not know the name of your Member of Congress, you can inquire locally at the Federal Building in your city, at the public library, at the city headquarters of the political parties, or at the city desk of a daily newspaper. Or you can send your research query addressed to one Congressman whose district you know covers part of the city in question, specify the address you are concerned with, and ask that your inquiry be forwarded if you have sent it to the wrong Congressional office. This is a routine courtesy on Capitol Hill.

4. CHAMBERS OF COMMERCE, TOURIST BUREAUS. For information on localities, especially economic data, and for generous supplies of printed matter designed to attract industry and tourists, Chambers of Commerce in many cities are highly efficient. Some chambers act directly as information agencies. Others have set up information offices operating under various names, such as visitors' bureau, convention bureau, tourist bureau, etc. It can be fairly presumed that there is an active chamber of commerce in most towns of any size in the United States. If you are in doubt, the Chamber of Commerce of the United States, 1615 H Street, N.W., Washington, D.C. 20036 can tell you.

5. TRADE ASSOCIATIONS. One of the primary functions of trade associations, a loose term for groups of people and businesses engaged in the same or similar economic activity, is gathering and supplying information about the industry. Frequently trade association statistics and studies are the only definitive ones in their particular fields. Although a small amount of trade association information is confidential, for members only, most of it is open to anyone who asks.

A national trade association is best approached through its chief executive officer, whose exact title varies widely among trade associations. Others to whom the researcher can best direct queries are the public relations director, the editor of the trade association publication, and the librarian at the association headquarters.

Sources from which to locate trade associations:

(a) The *Encyclopedia of Associations*, published by Gale Research Co., Detroit (see p. 50), which is alphabetized by the *key word* in the association title (National *RESTAURANT* Association is under "R", instead of "N"). This makes it possible to find out quickly whether or not there is an association devoted to a given activity.

(b) Indexed under "Associations," the *World Almanac* lists trade associations briefly, together with other groups. The listing includes name, address, number of members and founding date.

(c) *National Trade and Professional Associations of the U.S. and Canada and Labor Unions* is a large format paperbound book published annually by Columbia Books, Inc., 734 15th Street, N.W., Washington, D.C. 20005. Commercially oriented toward convention business, this directory can be found in hotels and local Chambers of Commerce, as well as in business collections in libraries.

6. EMBASSIES, LEGATIONS, U.N. DELEGATIONS. For information about places and events in countries other than the United States, a prime source is the diplomatic mission of the country in question. Every government with whom the United States maintains diplomatic relations has at its embassy or legation in Washington, D.C., an officer designated as press attaché, or someone who acts in that capacity. The press attaché is, in effect, the public relations officer for the mission. His office may answer queries directly, or may refer them to specialists in the mission, such as the cultural attaché or the commercial attaché.

In New York City the delegations of the various countries to the United Nations also have press attachés. Some are better equipped than others to answer queries beyond the U.N. activity of their countries. The researcher must try them for himself, and go to the Washington office if the U.N. mission in New York cannot help.

Certain foreign governments have also set up a library and information service in midtown New York, separate from the diplomatic missions, to cater to researchers whose questions relate to travel, history, commerce and other nondiplomatic subjects. Notable among these are the British Information Services and their counterparts maintained by the other governments of the British Commonwealth. Their libraries and staffs are excellent. To find these information offices in New York and Washington, look in the telephone directory under "British," "French," "Australian," etc. Or inquire from the U.N. mission or the embassy in Washington whether there is an information office where you can direct your queries.

7. ALUMNI OFFICES. Universities, colleges and preparatory schools are keeping more voluminous records on their alumni than ever before, because alumni have become a prime source for donations. Alumni bulletins and magazines contain a wealth of biographical material *unpublished elsewhere* on graduates of significance, and articles by or about such people *not indexed elsewhere*. Therefore the alumni secretary and his/her staff are prime sources of biographical information — including leads to many people who knew the subject intimately in his or her formative student years.

In some cases alumni secretaries protect the privacy of individuals by referring queries about a current address directly to the alumnus, to answer if he or she pleases. But usually queries about graduates of distinction are promptly answered, because the school takes pride in its alumni.

Research Gold in File Cabinets

See First:
    Finding Special Libraries in Your City (p. 22)
    Trade Associations (p. 78)
    Finding the Person Who Knows (p. 82)

A great deal of written material useful in serious research is preserved in file cabinets in thousands of accessible places. Yet to find and use these files we must search in ways different from those used to locate material in books and periodicals. Files contain just about anything on paper. There are printed pamphlets, folders, brochures and other publications too slim to be classified as books (which means forty-nine pages in the United States). There are publications for limited distribution (such as the news bulletin of an organization) which are not registered with the U.S. Copyright Office, not sold through bookstores, and not listed or cataloged anywhere. Mixed in with them may be: tear-sheets of individual magazine articles that *are* indexed by the H. W. Wilson Co. (see p. 49); pictorial material; leaflets; programs; manuscripts (see p. 102) that were never duplicated; and scrapbooks of clippings, pictures and mementos kept by an individual. The contents and organization of such mixed files vary from one extreme to the other.

You can waste time searching at random for files that may be highly useful to you, or you may overlook rich sources in file cabinets that you might have found with ease. Here are several ways to locate files that seem most promising — after which you are on your own in digging into them:

1. *Organizations.* Following the rule of "Who would care?" (see p. 10), look for the organizations, associations, companies, and so forth that would most likely be concerned with the subject in which you are interested. To find associations consult the *Encyclopedia of Associations* (p. 50); for manufacturing companies consult *Thomas Register* (p. 59). Companies generally keep their records under careful control on their own premises, but they frequently permit authorized students, biographers and historians to consult them. A company may require the researcher to agree to a company review of what he intends to publish, as a condition for permitting him to use the files at all. In this case the researcher must use his diplomatic skills to make the best arrangement he can.

With associations, access to records is generally easier. A researcher should check to see if the association has kept the files of the headquarters staff, annual meetings, officers and committees dealing with the subject of his inquiry. In many cases associations are glad to open their files to a serious researcher, especially if your study offers promise of reflecting favorably on the organization. Check also whether they have passed their back files on, perhaps for lack of storage space, to a related organization, to a parent federation, or to a library specializing in that subject. In these days of high rents in office buildings it occurs frequently that an organization cleans out its noncurrent files and turns them over to a nearby nonprofit educational institution, such as a university library.

2. *Special Libraries.* Librarians usually refer to their file collections (other than books, periodicals and manuscripts) as "vertical files," and indicate the extent of their holdings by the number of VFDs (vertical file drawers) on hand. When you consult a directory of special libraries in your metropolitan area, it is useful to check the VFD item and relate it to the number of volumes of books on hand, and the number of periodicals to which the library subscribes. The critical questions then are: How well are the files organized and indexed? Do they contain material specifically on the point of your research? A telephone query may save you a trip; and if you have a choice, it is the better organized collection, rather than the larger one, that is preferable for the first look. Although an alert, well-trained librarian can help you reach your research target, there is no substitute for examining the files yourself.

Frequently the files of an organization and the definitive special library files in a given field are one and the same. For instance, the Blaustein Library at the American Jewish Committee headquarters in New York has a vast collection of reference materials on intergroup relations, prejudice and discrimination, civil rights and civil liberties, human rights, left- and right-wing extremism, church-state relations in the U.S., Jewish community relations, and current problems of concern to the Jewish community in the U.S. The Blaustein Library has 40 vertical file drawers of reference materials, in addition to about 37,000 books and 700 periodicals.

3. *Public and University Libraries.* Public libraries, most of which are general libraries, usually do not have big vertical file collections because the materials are difficult to preserve and control. One exception is material on local history, which in many cities is given to the public library, and which the library staff feels

duty-bound to store, although the library is often not equipped to process it and preserve it according to professional library standards.

University libraries, like city libraries, are sometimes given files by graduates of the university and they feel it their duty to keep them, although the materials fall in a twilight zone between bound books (which are cataloged by author, title and subject) and manuscripts (which are organized by the former owner's name). File drawers are often tied closely by name to manuscript collections, and represent the documents and papers *other than correspondence* that accompanied a bequest of letters to the library.

4. *Personal Files*. Whenever you find a specialist or an expert, the chances are you have found someone who keeps personal files. An individual who has filed diligently and well in the subject-matter field in which you are interested is worth his weight in gold — provided he is willing to share his knowledge and his accumulations with you.

When you find such a person, be sure to ask him whether he has kept a *scrapbook* of newspaper clippings, book reviews and other excerpts from printed matter about himself and his work. If he or a proud member of his family has collected such a scrapbook (or the equivalent in looseleaf form) and if you are given access to it, you may have hit the research jackpot. For a good scrapbook contains material that is almost impossible to duplicate by research at a later date.

Personal files are worth pursuing well after the death of the individual who kept them. Frequently surviving families do not know just what to do with the files kept by the deceased, either in the home or in the office, so they postpone a decision by simply storing them. Therefore, the attics and basements of widows and children are well worth the researcher's attention.

Finding the Person Who Knows

See First:
Public Relations Sources (p. 42)
Associations — Key to Finding Specialists (p. 60)
Information Networks at Your Service (p. 75)
Biographical Reference: a Few Useful Books (p. 54)

Frequently the facts we want and need to know are not in print, but we have reason to believe that someone, an expert or a specialist, has them. The research job then is to locate that person. Here are a few ways to go about locating the person or persons who can help you:

1. *Organizations and Interest Groups.* If you do not already know it, find the association to which the expert or specialist is likely to belong through the *Encyclopedia of Associations* (p. 50). Through the association, or its regional or local division in your area, or a well informed local member, you can frequently locate someone with the special knowledge you require who is conveniently close to you.

Remember that those with particular interests or work specialties come into contact with others in their fraternity, or hear about them. So if a first referral turns out to be not what you need, one specialist can refer you to another. Physicians, for example, join the county medical society and also the organization (board or college) of their medical specialty. They read the medical journal articles written by their colleagues and meet them at professional meetings. Tournament caliber tennis players meet one another on the court, and keep up with the records of competitors in their specialized journal, *World Tennis.* Serious bridge players do the same. University and school teachers know many of their colleagues in other institutions through job transfers and professional groups.

Frequently an organization's membership roster is in print. Searching for such printed lists, and searching the lists for the people you want, is a first step. If an organization does not have a published membership directory, the officers or staff of the group will often help locate a member from the office files if the request appears legitimate and does not violate the member's privacy.

A roster of committee chairmen and committee members is highly useful in pinning down the names of those people in a national organization who have special interests and knowledge. The organization's annual report or its official publication can be a quick guide to the names of committee chairmen.

2. *Specialized News Reporters and Editors* (see p. 75). The specialized reporter on the local newspaper, if he or she is a good one, can guide the researcher to people near at hand who are the sources for newspaper articles — in business, or politics, or the courts, or medicine, or local history. The reporter or editor may therefore be a shortcut to finding the expert you need, or finding a local member of a national organization who may have its

membership roster, annual report, official publication and other material of help.

3. *Business Card File.* I have found that one of the most effective ways to keep in touch with people I have met once, and whom I regard as potential sources of specialized information, is to keep a file of their business cards. (This is just a stack of cards held together with rubber bands). Frequently after one casual contact I quickly forget the person's name, but I do remember that he was a certain kind of specialist, or connected with a certain organization. For this reason I do not file the business cards alphabetically, but rather by date received, and mark the date on the card. I note carefully on each card the important facts about that person, such as his fields of knowledge and where, or through whom, we met. This enables me to call on him with a request for research help long after our meeting, even though I had forgotten his name in the interim. If he does not have a card, I write the information down on a piece of stiff paper cut to business-card size and file it with the rest.

This is a mixed lot of names and identities held together merely by the fact of our having met and exchanged cards once. But it has helped me time and again to reach people who are somewhat flattered to learn that they were remembered after a long interval.

4. *Going to the Horse's Mouth.* In research in fields where there are experts aplenty, we sometimes overlook the testimony of the ordinary person — not a scholar or an expert in the accepted sense — who knows certain limited things because he was there, he was personally involved, he did it himself. The serious researcher should always seek out such witnesses because they can frequently correct a record that was distorted in the first writing, and was perpetuated by scholarly experts copying each other.

Going to the horse's mouth has proved especially valuable to contemporary historians and biographers, because eyewitnesses and participants have memories of things not previously in print. They have helped us get a more accurate picture, for instance, of such past events as the sinking of the *Titanic* in 1912, the Scopes ("Monkey") Trial of 1925, and the Japanese attack on Pearl Harbor in 1941. In addition to ordinary observers, such people as the chauffeur, the doorman, the secretary, the executive assistant and the switchboard operator observe people and events from a special viewpoint. They should therefore be considered prime sources for the researcher — as they are for the detective.

One step removed are professionals such as the physician, attorney, clergyman and tax accountant who have special, intimate knowledge touching people of interest to historians and biographers, and who are bound by professional ethics to keep confidences. But even with them, the passage of time permits a certain relaxation of the confidentiality rule for the sake of contributing to an accurate historical record.

Query Letters That Get Results

When you write a letter to a potential source of research information, write in the way in which you would appreciate being written to. Especially when the recipient does not know the writer, it is unfair to put him to unnecessary trouble to assist you. It is also unrealistic. You are most likely to receive a satisfactory reply if you observe these rules of correspondence in research:

1. *Be precise.* Ask the source-person exactly what you want from him, putting your query within the context of what you have already learned, what readings you have done, etc. This will help your correspondent see that all you want from him is a brief, precise answer. And it will avoid his troubling to supply information you already have. For instance, do *not* ask an expert for a list of books to read on your subject; instead, send him your bibliography and ask if there are any obvious important omissions that he can call to your attention.

2. *Ask for printed matter.* After outlining what you want to know, particularly when corresponding with public information officers and public relations people, ask if they have printed matter that would help in your research, which they can mail to you. If so, then you can first read what is sent and follow up later with a more precise query.

3. *Be diplomatic.* When seeking information from an expert or a Very Important Personage, write a convincing explanation of why that person alone can help you. Possible ploys in correspondence might resemble these: "After much study of the subject I have been unable to find any written reference to _____, so I turn to you as the only surviving person who was involved . . ." or: "I can find no reference in all your writings, the definitive ones on the subject, to _____. So I ask you now. . . ."

Remember that it does no harm to butter up the expert and the VIP, if it is done discreetly and with sincerity.

4. *Correspond with authors.* Writers of books and articles frequently receive letters commenting on their work from people anxious to get into the act by supplying the author with more information. This happens especially with contemporary history and biography. Thus, the author gathers unsolicited, additional material after publication that he wishes he had acquired before his work went to press. If you correspond with the authors of books and articles that you are using in your research work, you may elicit fresh material, never in print, which came to the authors in this way. That is, if they are willing to share it.

Interviewing

See First:
Finding the Person Who Knows (p. 82)

One of the best expositions of interviewing methods in print (known to the author) is the twenty-five-page chapter on interviewing in *A Treasury of Tips for Writers*, edited by Marvin Weisbord, published by the *Writer's Digest*, 22 East 12th Street, Cincinnati, Ohio 45201. This chapter consists of thirty-two short sections contributed by some of the most accomplished professional magazine and book writers in the United States. It is slanted toward interviewing as a research technique for book and magazine article material, but that fact does not diminish the value of these tips to those who do interviewing for other purposes. *Subject Guide to Books in Print* (see p. 32) lists dozens of books on interviewing for various purposes, such as employment, journalism, psychiatry, social case work and others, so there is plenty of available reading on the subject. The best way to become a good interviewer, however, is to practice — and to learn from your mistakes as well as from your successes.

Obtaining information by interview is an art in itself. Some people will always find it difficult because they do not have the kind of personality that invites interviewees to talk freely and frankly. To others with an outgoing nature that inspires confidence, even intimacy, interviewing comes easily and naturally. Whatever kind of person a researcher may be, however, he can become a more effective interviewer by following certain basic rules.

1. *Do your homework first.* It is a waste of your time, and insulting to the interviewee, to ask him questions which you could have

answered yourself by advance preparation. Concentrate instead on filling gaps in the written record by asking the person why he decided or did certain things. Or ask his opinions on subjects where they are not known. Let him respect you for having done your homework before you called on him for assistance.

2. *Establish your relationship with the interviewee.* You get the best results from an interview by letting your subject know just who you are, and your purpose in interviewing him. Only then will he feel relaxed in answering questions and confident in telling you things he might not take the time to tell others. If at all possible, try to give him a reason why his cooperating in the interview will fulfill some interest of his, such as helping obtain recognition for a relative or an old friend for an important accomplishment — or even for himself.

3. *Let the interviewee talk.* Ask your questions, then try to intrude as little as possible, except to direct your subject in speaking to the points on which you want information. It is better to let him ramble than for you, the interviewer, to do too much of the talking. The purpose of the interview, after all, is for you to draw information from him, and not the other way around.

4. *Write down your interview record immediately.* Whether you take shorthand notes during an interview, or write longhand, or use a recorder, it is important to write out the record of an interview as soon as possible. The reason is that no one's record is complete, and you can interpolate items that you remember. The act of transcribing the interview when it is fresh in your mind helps you to fill gaps and correct errors. It also reminds you of possible further questions, which you may be able to put to your subject at another meeting or by telephone.

When your transcript is complete it is often productive to supply the interviewee with a copy. He may catch some errors, and he may even enlarge on what he told you during the interview.

C. ADVANCED TECHNIQUES

Search Out the Trade Press

See First:
   Finding Special Libraries in Your City (p. 22)
   Periodical Indexes: the Two Levels (p. 29)
   Your Trade or Professional Directory (p. 36)
   Trade Associations (p. 78)

The specialized trade press is a rich source of detailed information for the researcher. For the most part it is commercial, being slanted toward news and advertising aimed to help people in the same economic activity, or specialists engaged in similar work, to perform more efficiently, to cut costs and thus to prosper economically. Examples: *Variety*, the weekly journal of show business, that is read by theatre operators, actors, musicians and everyone connected with the stage or screen; *Flying*, edited for pilots and plane owners active in general aviation; and *Literary Market Place*, the annual business directory of American book publishing. There is a press for virtually every interest group in the country — professionals, businessmen, craftsmen or specialists in one line of work — whether they are organized or not. Closely allied to the trade press is the hobbyist's press, which the hobbyist does not read for economic gain, but which is definitely published for that purpose.

Ltd., Box 3552, New York, N.Y. 10017.

CITY DIRECTORIES OF BLACK BUSINESSES
City directories of black businesses are listed alphabetically by State and City. Address of the publisher is included. National directories of special types of black businesses are also listed. 5 pp. Institute for Minority Business Education, Howard U, 2345 Sherman Ave. NW, Washington, D.C. 20001. Free.

DIRECTORY OF AFRO AMERICAN RESOURCES
A list of organizations and institutions holding research materials in Afro-American studies. Includes ... zations. ... city, an ... cities. ... with 4,! ... Bowker ... York, N ...

DIRECTORY OF BLACK BUSINESSES IN MICHIGAN
Over 1,000 names of black-owned or managed businesses and the name of the owner/manager. Arranged alphabetically by city. 85 pp. The University of Michigan Industrial Development Division, 2200 North Campus Blvd., Ann Arbor, Mich. 48105. Free.

DIRECTORY OF BLACK LITERARY MAGAZINES
Details information of black literary magazines in the United States. Minority Research Center Inc., 117 R St. N.E., Washington, D.C. 20002.

A DIRECTORY OF BLACK-OWNED BUSINESSES IN WASHINGTON, D.C.
A list of about 2,500 businesses owned by black entrepreneurs in the District of Columbia. Arranged alphabetically by kind of business with address, phone number and name of owner. 75 pp. Institute for Minority Business Education. P.O. Box 748, Howard University, Washington, D.C. 20059. Free.

DIRECTORY OF ETHNIC PUBLISHERS AND RESOURCE
Provides an alphabetical and categorical listing of 300 organizations and publishers with strong or exclusive interests in ethnic and minority material. 90 pp. American Library Association, 50 E. Huron St., Chicago, Ill. 60611.

minority architectural and engineering firms, including address, phone, firm size, services, etc. American Consulting Engineers Council, 1155 15th St. N.W., Washington, D.C. 20005.

DIRECTORY OF MINORITY BUSINESS RESOURCES OF THE AMERICAN MARKETING ASSOCIATION
Provides information regarding the American Marketing Association volunteers who are available to work with minority businessmen 100 pp. Office of Minority Business Enterprise Commerce Department, Washington, D.C. Free

DIRECTORY OF NATIONAL BLACK ORGANIZATIONS
... listing of national ... ons in the areas o. ... cational, religious ... upational, political ... m Associates, Inc ... N.Y. 10037. $5.00

> When a researcher wants to find out whether there is a published directory on a certain subject, the answer can be found in the **Guide to American Directories**.

A DIRECTORY OF SPANISH - SPEAKING NEW YORK
6,000 entries arranged alphabetically in 100 categories. Includes businesses, services, manufacturers, distributors, retailers, churches schools, lawyers, physicians, pharmacies restaurants, government offices, community organizations, newspapers, magazines, radio T.V., etc. serving the two million residents o Hispanic background in the New York metropolitan area. 340 bilingual pp. Quadrangle Books, c/o The New York Times, P.O. Box 590, Yonkers, N.Y. 10702.

DIRECTORY OF SPECIAL PROGRAMS FOR MINORITY GROUP MEMBERS: CAREER INFORMATION SERVICES, EMPLOYMENT SKILLS BANKS, FINANCIAL AID SOURCE
Lists over 750 national and local organizations 300 Federally-funded programs, and hundred sponsored by individual colleges and universities providing special help to Black, Hispanic Asian American, and American India candidates, their counselors and prospective employers, including 150 programs develope especially for women both entering an reentering education and employment. 400 pp Garrett Park Press, Garrett Park, Marylan 20766. $9.75.

DIRECTORY OF WOMEN AND MINORITY MEN IN ACADEMIC JOURNALISM COMMUNICATION
Contains an alphabetical listi...

The trade press is frequently overlooked in research, or not given the attention it is worth, for several reasons. Among them is the fact that academics generally do not inform students that there is such a thing as the trade press, or dismiss it as unscholarly. In addition, because the readership of most trade periodicals is such a specialized group, general libraries can afford to carry only a small proportion of them, and indexes to periodicals cover only a small selection of them. There are so many specialized trade journals, magazines and newsletters published in the United States, and so many new ones appear each year while others disappear by merger, that no list can be completely up-to-date. But there are a number of ways to find the standard trade press sources for a given inquiry.

For DIRECTORIES, many of which are annuals, the best source is the *Guide to American Directories*, edited by Bernard Klein, published by B. Klein Publications, P.O. Box 8503, Coral Springs, Florida 33065. This guide bears the descriptive subtitle: *A guide to the major business directories of the United States, covering all industrial, professional, and mercantile categories.* If your library has it, here is a sound first step in pursuing the trade press. The directories to which it leads often carry advertising for other reference sources, such as trade periodicals and newsletters.

For PERIODICALS there are two useful directories, in which the trade press is mingled alphabetically by subject field with noncommercial periodicals. One is the *Standard Periodical Directory* (described on p. 60), which lists American and Canadian periodicals only. The other is *Ulrich's International Periodicals Directory* (R. R. Bowker), which does not list so many periodicals, but which lists titles from other countries in all parts of the world. Neither of these directories is free of errors by omission, as I have determined by finding at times a certain title in one of them but not in the other. For thoroughness in one subject field I generally prefer the *Standard Periodical Directory*. But when I want to find specialized periodicals from England, France, Australia or other countries relevant to my search there is no handy substitute for *Ulrich's*.

For NEWSLETTERS, the best single source is the *National Directory of Newsletters and Reporting Services*, published by Gale Research Company, Detroit, Mich. (see p. 50). In order to examine the files of specialized newsletters (even more than with magazines and directories) you must either subscribe to them, or rely on specialized libraries, or find an individual in your city who has his own file of back copies (see below in this section).

1166   MOTION PICTURES

778.5   IT
FILMSTUDIO SETTANTA.* 1974. m. free.
Filmstudio 70, Via Orti d'Alibert, 1c, Rome, Italy.
film rev. illus. circ. 7,000.

791.43   GW
FILMTHEATER-PRAXIS - WERBUNG HEUTE.
1954. m. DM.15. Kommanditgesellschaft Verlag
Horst Axtmann GmbH und Co., Wilhelmstr. 42,
6200 Wiesbaden, W. Germany (B.R.D.) Ed. Horst
Axtmann. adv. bk. rev.
    Formerly: Filmtheater-Praxis (ISSN 0015-1742)

791.43   US   ISSN 0362-0905
FOCUS: CHICAGO. 1967. bi-m. $2 to non-members.
Facets Multimedia, Inc., 1517 W. Fullerton Ave.,
Chicago, IL 60614. Ed. Nicole Dreiske. adv. bk.
rev. film rev. illus. circ. 2,400.

7?
FOC
1?
U
C
fil
U

FOR THE TIME BEING. see LITERATURE

791.43   YU   ISSN 0015-8704
FOTO-KINO REVIJA; jugoslovenski casopis za
fotografijui amaterski film. (Text in Serbocroatian)
1948. m. 72 din.($5) Tehnicka Knjiga. 7. Jula 26,
Belgrade, Yugoslavia. Ed. Zivojin Jeremic.
    Latin alphabet

FOTOCAMARA CON POPULAR
PHOTOGRAPHY. see PHOTOGRAPHY

FOTOKINO-MAGAZIN. see PHOTOGRAPHY

FOTOMUNDO. see PHOTOGRAPHY

FOTON; fotografia, cine y sonida (photography,
amateur movie and sound) see PHOTOGRAPHY

FOTOTRIBUNE; maandblad voor fotografie, smalfilm
en geluid. see PHOTOGRAPHY

791.43   BE   ISSN 0015-9786
FRANCIS BOLEN'S NEWSLETTER. 1952. m. 250
Fr. Francis Bolen, Ed. & Pub., 30 rue de l'Etuve,
1000 Brussels, Belgium. film rev. bibl. circ. 1,000.
(tabloid format)

778.5   HK
FRESH/CHING HSIN.* 1973. m. Fresh Productions
- Ching Hsin Chih Tso Kung Ssu Chu Pan Pu,
Room 11a, 11th Floor, 30-32 Queen's Rd. East,
Hong Kong, Hong Kong. illus.

GAZZETTA DEl·   see ART

GES?   ee MUS?

791.43   AG   ISSN 0046-7286
HERALDO DEL CINE. 1931. fortn. Montevideo 443,
Buenos Aires, Argentina. adv. illus. index.
cum.index. circ. 5,000. (tabloid format)

HISPANICAMERICAN ARTS; reference magazine to
the hispanicamerican arts. see THEATER

917   US   ISSN 0018-3660
HOLLYWOOD REPORTER. 1930. d. $30. c/o Tichi
Wilkerson Miles, 6715 Sunset Blvd., Hollywood,
CA 90028. Ed. Ralph Kaminsky. adv. bk. rev. film
rev. play rev. (tabloid format)

791.43   HU   ISSN 0018-7798
HUNGAROFILM BULLETIN. (Text in English,
French and German) 1965. 5/yr. free. Hungarofilm,
Bathory u. 10. Budapest 5. Hungary. film rev. circ.

The special value of **Ulrich's International Periodicals
Directory** lies in its listings of specialized periodicals,
by subject categories, from all parts of the world.

?12
?r for
?.
?w
?t
Sunshine. adv. film rev. illus. index. circ. 14,500.

791.43   SI   ISSN 0019-5979
INDIAN MOVIE NEWS. (Text in English & Tamil)
1952. m. S.$20.20. Chinese Pictorial Review Ltd,
112-120 Robinson Road, Singapore, Singapore. Ed.
I. S. Menon. film rev. circ. 36,000. (processed)

792   GW   ISSN 0046-9343
INFORMATION G. 1970. bi-m. free. Wolfgang
Gielow Verlag, Theatinerstr. 35, 8000 Munich 2, W.
Germany (B. R. D.) Ed.Bd. bk. rev. bibl.

574 610   GW   ISSN 0073-8417
INSTITUT FUER DEN WISSENSCHAFTLICHEN
FILM. PUBLIKATIONEN ZU
WISSENSCHAFTLICHEN FILMEN. SEKTION
BIOLOGIE. (Text in German; summaries in English
and French) 1963. 4/yr. DM.7 per issue. Institut
fuer den Wissenschaftlichen Film, Nonnenstieg 72,
3400 Goettingen, W. Germany (B.R.D.) Ed. G.
Wolf.

301.16   CN   ISSN 0020-4927
INTER; information et documentation sur les moyens
de communication sociale. 1967. m. Can.$12. Office
des Communications Sociales, 4635 rue de Lorimer,
Montreal, Que. H2H 2B4, Canada. Ed. Lucien
Labelle. circ. 500-600.

INTERNATIONAL ALLIANCE OF THEATRICAL
STAGE EMPLOYEES AND MOVIN?
MACHINE OPERA?   ?F T?
S?

Another way to start is to consult the specialized periodicals index published by H. W. Wilson Co. (see p. 49) that in your judgment comes closest to your field of inquiry. By examining the list of periodical titles inside the front cover you can find a few titles of magazines and journals that cover your field in general, or come close to it. By examining copies of these (and for this you may have to visit a specialized library) you may find references to other publications in the field, and advertisements for them. Certainly the editors of periodicals of broader coverage, which Wilson is likely to index, know about the others of narrower scope with which they compete, or from which they draw information for their own use.

Still another starting point is with companies, organizations and associations, through which you can find the specialists who would know their own trade press. The researcher can then go directly to his target by asking the specialized craftsman, or professional, or businessman:

"What trade journals do you read? Which ones do your colleagues read? Which are your best printed sources of information?" and, "Do you have copies of them?"

Ask specifically about magazines, journals, newsletters and directories. This personal approach is often more productive than trying to track down highly specialized trade publications in libraries, where most of them are not to be found. The total circulation of a specialized trade journal may be only 20,000, with only a few hundred subscribers in your city. In this case the public library may never have been asked to subscribe to a journal so specialized, and the librarians have not heard of it. Go instead to the practitioner who needs the trade press in his work, and ask him.

The Librarian's Guide to Reference Books

See First:
   The Best Guide to Reference Books (p. 24)
   Finding Reference Books in Libraries (p. 25)
   Know the Reference Book Catalogs (p. 49)
   Biographical Reference: a Few Useful Books (p. 54)
   Reference Books That Open New Doors (p. 57)

The standard work in which librarians look up reference book titles to suggest to readers is Eugene P. Sheehy's *Guide to Reference Books* (Chicago, American Library Association). For many years this guide was known among professional librarians as *Winchell*, after its veteran editor, Constance M. Winchell. Now it is more commonly termed *Sheehy* after her successor. By whichever nickname it is called by the librarian you deal with, this is the Bible of the reference librarian's trade, since it is published by the American Library Association. From the first semester in library science school the librarian is taught to turn to it when a researcher asks for source books.

Because it is a comprehensive work of 1,000 two-column pages containing only brief descriptions of books on all kinds of subjects, no librarian can be expected to master its contents. Nor can she give a sound judgment of the value of many of the books listed under a given subject in *Sheehy-Winchell*. But an experienced reference librarian can help the reader find the headings and pages he wants in it, then turn it over to him.

It is worth the time of every serious research worker to inspect this source and to become generally familiar with its contents and organization. There are biennial supplements published by the A.L.A. between editions, and the reference librarian should be asked for whatever supplements are available. When the researcher takes up a new subject, he can check *Sheehy-Winchell* under the headings relevant to his work and note the reference books that may be useful. By inspecting these early in his project he may save time by finding that someone else has already collected and put into print the material he wants.

A British guide, similar to *Sheehy-Winchell* but based on British reference books, is *The Guide to Reference Material*, edited by Arthur J. Walford, assisted by L. M. Payne and C. A. Toase (London, The Library Association; New York, R. R. Bowker).

Using the National Union Catalog

See First:
Using the Library of Congress (p. 73)
Your Congressman Can Help (p. 68)

The National Union Catalog in the Library of Congress, Washington, D.C., is a register to help you find out what libraries have certain books you want to consult. It consists of a card file that is open to readers, located near the card catalog of LC holdings but separate from it, on the East side of the LC main building, at First and East Capitol streets SE, opposite the Capitol.

The National Union Catalog (NUC) does contain cards for books that are widely held in libraries. Its primary purpose is to help readers find those out-of-print books that are relatively rare. For each book the NUC has an author card only — no title or subject cards. The NUC has assigned a short letter-code to more than 1,100 reference libraries and each card is marked with the letter-code of the libraries where it is known that the book is in the collection. Thus, a card marked with the codes *CU, DNIH* and *ICA* indicates that copies of that book are known to be at the University of California, Berkeley; at the U.S. National Institutes of Health Library, Bethesda, Maryland; and at the Art Institute of Chicago Library. Most NUC cards have from one to twenty code marks. The book may be in other collections, as well, because additions are being made to them all the time, and there is a lag between their accession in a reference library and the addition of the code to the NUC cards.

The best way to consult the NUC, of course, is to go to Washington yourself. But this is impractical for most people. A second way is to have a friend living in Washington visit the LC and search the catalog for you. A third way is to ask your Congressman's office to request the LC staff to make the search (see p. 69) on the limits which the LC tries to place on service to Members of Congress acting for their constituents). The Congressman can then send you the information. A fourth way is to write directly to the Union Catalog Reference Unit, Library of Congress, Washington, D.C. 20540, stating your request clearly and specifically. If your letter clearly marks you as a serious, scholarly person and your search request will not take much time, they will try to help.

A fifth way to consult the NUC, and a tricky one, is to examine the printed, bound volumes in your local reference library in which the NUC cards are reproduced in reduced size, three columns to a page. However (and this is their weakness as a research resource) their contents have not been cumulated into one alphabetical series. A researcher must therefore be certain to consult all the series available before concluding that a book is not listed and giving up. In the case of a book published in recent years (since the 1950s), knowing the date of publication can speed your finding the entry in a recent NUC volume. It is more difficult for pre-1956 entries in the NUC. A new series of volumes combining all pre-1956 NUC cards in one alphabet is being edited and sold to libraries. Since 1955, the NUC has appeared in monthly, quarterly, annual and quinquennial issues.

All this means that this method of search is difficult, and you should ask the help of the best reference librarian if you have trouble. Of course, you may find the reproduced NUC card for which you are searching quickly; but if you should not find it, do not conclude that there is no entry for that book in the NUC in Washington. You should then employ one of the four search methods described above and check the NUC itself.

By consulting the National Union Catalog you may find that there is a copy of the book you want in a nearby library that you had not checked before. But if all known copies are at a distance too great for convenient visiting, you can obtain the book through the Interlibrary Loan system.

Now See:
Interlibrary Loan (p. 96)
Local Union Catalogs and Interlibrary Loan
    Programs (p. 98)

Interlibrary Loan

See First:
Using the National Union Catalog (p. 94)

Interlibrary Loan is a cooperative system by which libraries in all parts of the country lend specific books to one another on order, for the use of readers who have asked for them. The books are sent by mail, insured and registered, from the lending to the borrowing library, and usually must be used at the borrowing library. The reader who has requested a book by Interlibrary Loan may not take it home. The only cost to the reader is the postage and insurance fee.

In order to obtain a book through the Interlibrary Loan system you must first find out, from the National Union Catalog or other means, what library outside your own city has the book. Second, you must order a book through a local library that participates in the Interlibrary Loan system. (Not all libraries do — the New York City Public Library, for instance, participates only on a limited basis.) Third, you must use the book on the premises of the borrowing library within a limited time, after which it is returned.

The Library of Congress participates in Interlibrary Loan, but it will not lend a book that the reader can find closer to his home than Washington.

The writer has found the cost and restrictions in Interlibrary Loan to be minor in contrast to the advantages offered. When doing research in the Library of Congress in the late 1950s, I found that the National Union Catalog listed only two copies of a rare book I required — one at Chicago, the other at Yale. I ordered the Yale copy, received it in ten days, and used it for a week. Total cost to me was about one dollar.

The Center for Research Libraries (5721 Cottage Grove Avenue, Chicago, Ill. 60637) is a variation on the Interlibrary Loan principle. It is a research collection supported by its member institutions (180 academic, state, government and company libraries), from which materials are loaned for use by readers at the members' location. The Center holds more than 3,000,000 books, and such rarities on microfilm as trial transcripts, foreign doctoral dissertations and foreign newspapers. It usually works faster than Interlibrary Loan, and ships materials promptly in response to a collect telephone or teletype request.

Now See:
Obtaining Out-of-Print Books (p. 105)

Local Union Catalogs and Interlibrary Loan Programs

See First:
Using the National Union Catalog (p. 94)
Interlibrary Loan (p. 96)

You should make it a point to inquire whether the library you visit participates in either a local union catalog or a local interlibrary loan program. Frequently libraries in the process of instituting such services do not publicize them effectively, so you must take the initiative to find out.

As the number of books and periodicals that libraries are asked to furnish to readers rises faster than their budgets, libraries are increasingly turning to forms of cooperation with one another. Libraries within the same system (city, county or state) are working out ways to serve an expanded clientele with materials held by only one (or a few) of them. The same development is taking place within large universities that have many libraries, among independent schools and colleges in the same locality, and among town libraries.

In a local union catalog a reader can find out whether any of the nearby cooperating libraries holds a given book or periodical, and if so, which one. Allied to this there may be a local, or regional, interlibrary loan program, by which materials are shipped from one library in the group to another, in response to a reader's call for it.

A variation on the forms of cooperation described above is a periodical reprint service among cooperating libraries. In this case the library holding a scholarly periodical will, on order, send to the ordering library only a duplicated copy (by Xerox or other process) of the one article required — thus saving the cost of shipping the periodical out and back.

Buying Library of Congress Catalog Cards

To help researchers compile a bibliography on a specialized project, the Cataloging Distribution Service of the Library of Congress will sell by mail a packet of all LC catalog cards bearing a specified subject heading or classification number. The advantage of buying cards is to have at hand a list of all LC books on a given subject in this classification, and all information the cards contain, eliminating any chance of error in transmission.

To place an order the researcher must first find the LC subject heading by consulting *Subject Headings Used in the Dictionary*

Catalog of the Library of Congress, which may be kept in the local librarian's office. He can also get a quick clue to the subject headings and classification numbers directly from the cards in the local library card catalog. He should also consult (in a reference library) the books entitled *Library of Congress Classification Schedules,* to see whether there are other numbers covering books closely related to his subject, for which he might also want to order catalog cards. He should then write for price information to the Cataloging Distribution Service, Library of Congress, Building 159, Navy Yard Annex, Washington, D.C. 20541, stipulating his precise subject of investigation and its outer limits, with the classification numbers he wants. Pricing is essential, because the number of books under one classification number may range widely, and the price of the entire set of cards may be excessive. The answer to a query on the number of cards and the price will help the researcher order intelligently.

> *Now See:*
> *Using the National Union Catalog* (p. 94)
> *Classification Systems Can Help You* (p. 111)

Finding Unpublished Doctoral Dissertations

For many years the thousands of unpublished doctoral dissertations presented each year by candidates for the Ph.D. degree represented a huge untapped research resource. These papers were the fruit of a tremendous amount of work, particularly in the compilation of bibliography and in manuscript research. Yet until recently it was very difficult for all but the most specialized scholars to find out whether a doctoral dissertation had been written on a given subject, because most dissertations were not published. In most cases the Ph.D. candidate had deposited a bound typescript of the doctoral dissertation in the university library, and retained a copy at home. Most of us would never find our way to this work because it was not indexed anywhere as a published book.

Recently, however, University Microfilms International, a subsidiary of the Xerox Corporation (300 North Zeeb Road, Ann Arbor, Mich. 48106) has provided the keys to this great research resource. It does so through five services which were started at different times but which now fit into each other and form a system. They are:

1. *American Doctoral Dissertations,* a bound index widely available in research libraries, arranged by authors in subject fields,

and by institutions. Every dissertation accepted in North America is covered.

2. *Dissertation Abstracts International*, a monthly periodical containing the abstracts of Ph.D. dissertations accepted by universities throughout the world.

3. Copies of full dissertations, sold on demand, in either a microfilm or xerographic (paper) copy.

4. DATRIX II (*D*irect *A*ccess *t*o *R*eference *I*nformation: a Xerox service), a computerized query system that supplies dissertation bibliographic information for any designated area of interest or study, on demand.

5. *Comprehensive Dissertation Index*, a cumulative index covering the years since 1861, available in libraries.

To explain each of these:

1. The index *American Doctoral Dissertations*, found in reference libraries, is a quick but limited aid to finding the exact title, author, year and university of a particular dissertation. But it is useful only when some of the details are known. For instance, it can help pin down the date and title of a dissertation accepted by the Harvard History Department from a named person. It is useless as a way to find out whether anyone ever presented a dissertation at any university on a given subject.

2. Once a researcher has pinned down a certain dissertation title (with author and date) that interests him, he can then turn to the bound volumes of *Dissertation Abstracts International*, to which many reference libraries subscribe. Here he can read a 600-word abstract of the dissertation, prepared by the candidate at the time his dissertation was presented and supplied then to University Microfilms International (UMI) for distribution. From the abstract the researcher can decide whether or not he wants to read the entire dissertation.

3. The researcher can order an entire dissertation from University Microfilms International in one of two forms. Complete dissertations on 35 mm roll film are available at a modest price, and these can be read at any library equipped with a 35 mm microfilm reader. He can also order from UMI a xerographic copy made from the film, enlarged to about two-thirds the size of the original typescript pages, or about 5½ by 8½ inches. At this size they are

easy to read. The price for any dissertation in this form, no matter the size, is also reasonable.

4. The DATRIX II service has been in operation only since 1967. It is a computer-based retrieval system that helps the researcher locate whatever doctoral dissertations may be helpful in his work — WHEN HE DOES NOT KNOW AT THE OUTSET WHETHER ANY SUCH PAPERS HAVE EVEN BEEN WRITTEN. Once he finds titles that may be helpful, he can then consult the abstracts, to see if those that appear promising from their titles are worth further study. DATRIX II is a tremendous time-saver for the conscientious researcher, and makes accessible reference material that would otherwise not be found.

To use the DATRIX II service, the researcher must fill out an order form (available from UMI), on which he specifies the key words in dissertation titles that he wants the computer to select for him. A clearly written instruction sheet is furnished for his guidance. The basic charge for a DATRIX II search of the roughly 500,000 dissertations on file is modest.

5. The *Comprehensive Dissertation Index 1861-1972* is a 37-volume subject and author index to more than 400,000 dissertations accepted at American and Canadian universities since doctoral programs began. It is designed so that any dissertation or group of dissertations can be found conveniently. It cites references to abstracts in *Dissertation Abstracts International*, simplifying the finding of an abstract. Yearly supplements are published, each adding more than 35,000 references to the basic 37 volumes. Using this retrospective index is by far the easiest method of obtaining information either about a dissertation or even whether or not one had been written *primarily* on a particular subject. But for locating dissertations in related subject areas that may be useful, the DATRIX II system casts a wider net because it employs several key words in each title, whereas the *Comprehensive Index* is based on only one key word.

There is literally no other way to search this huge mass of unpublished dissertations presented at more than 250 institutions around the world. Although it started with U.S. dissertations dating from 1938, UMI has expanded its data base to include European dissertations.

Now See:
University Microfilms International (p. 110)

Digging into Manuscripts and Papers

See First:
Research Gold in File Cabinets (p. 80)
Finding the Person Who Knows (p. 82)

There comes a time in many a research project when printed sources will no longer do, and you must look for information in original handwritten or typewritten documents. The most fruitful place to hunt for them is in research libraries. Historians usually call such documents "original sources"; librarians use the term "manuscripts." Both historians and librarians also use the term "papers" — under which they group letters, notes, diaries, business accounts, logbooks, reports, drafts, and so forth. In some cases papers may have been copied in longhand by clerks or duplicated (by letterpress or carbon copy) in very small numbers, but have not been generally distributed.

Research in manuscript collections is always a challenge, because you never know what you will find, or whether you will find what you want. In a sense, a day spent examining papers in a manuscript collection is like a day's fishing; you do not know whether you will end the day with a good catch or go home empty-handed. But for excitement it far exceeds reading material in print because you have the sense of discovery, of being there first. In fact, this very excitement can lead the researcher down fascinating paths away from his subject, and if he does not guard himself against distractions he can lose sight of his original purpose in digging into the papers.

The first step in manuscript work is to find out whether there are any collections of papers likely to be helpful in your research, and if so, where they are. Useful manuscripts may be found in the hands of private individuals (see p. 82), or in the files of organizations (p. 80). But for those that are held by libraries and other repositories, the following two sources are of considerable value:

1. *A Guide to Archives and Manuscripts in the United States*, edited by Philip M. Hamer (Yale University Press, 1961). Prepared under the sponsorship of the U.S. National Historical Publications Committee, Hamer's guide is a well-organized, one-volume directory that helps the researcher find all the manuscript collections concerned with a certain person or subject — that were known to the editor in 1961, when this guide was published. Because it is steadily becoming dated, however, its value for more recent subjects is limited.

2. *National Union Catalog of Manuscript Collections*, published by the Library of Congress. Building on the principle of Hamer's guide and, in effect, superseding it, this NUCMC (as the Library of Congress terms it) consists of a series of volumes published roughly once a year since 1962. The cumulative index in the latest volume shows the reader where in the preceding volumes he can find descriptions of particular collections. The main body of each book consists of reproduced catalog cards bringing together in one series scattered information about manuscript material.

Once you have located a certain collection of papers and have arrived at the library where they are deposited, it is always valuable to find out from the supervisor of the manuscript collection whether there is an index, guide or "register" (the terms vary) to assist you. Unless she is asked, a library assistant may fail to inform you that a typewritten guide to the contents of the papers is available. So you should routinely ask whether there is a register to the collection. In large collections using a register is a great time-saver, because papers relating to a given subject may be scattered through many years of a collection of letters that is organized chronologically. Or they may be grouped together because the person whose papers you are examining may have kept his files that way. There are mixed views among manuscript curators as to methods of organization of collections; consequently there is no uniformity. Frequently manuscript collections are left as they were when they were given to the repository — organized in part by subject, in part alphabetically by name of correspondent, and in part chronologically. It is up to the researcher to find his way, and a register can save a great deal of needle-in-haystack hunting.

An important part of the technique of manuscript research lies in thinking carefully about which people, and which organizations, would have been concerned with the subject of your research. Then look for their papers. For a biography of Justice Thurgood Marshall of the United States Supreme Court, for instance, it would make sense to look for the papers of John W. Davis. Davis, 1924 Democratic candidate for President, was the attorney who argued the segregationist side of the public school appeal to the Supreme Court in 1953, against Marshall, who argued successfully for public school desegregation. Here (from carbon copies of outgoing letters) you may find what Davis wrote to his close friends about Marshall, and what others wrote to Davis in comment on his opponent.

Research into manuscripts of a few very distinguished figures is being simplified by their being published and indexed. For example, the papers of Woodrow Wilson are a Princeton University project, and the Benjamin Franklin papers are being prepared for publications at Yale. *Subject Guide to Books in Print* (see p. 32) can guide you to such published collections. But most of the collections indexed in the NUCMC are the papers of relatively minor figures in American life. Their number will increase in the next few years because librarians ambitious to build their collections actively solicit them. Manuscript collections are therefore sure to become an ever richer source of information for research workers in many lines of inquiry. They are no longer restricted to the papers left by notables, but now include the papers of specialists, professionals, and those whose relationship to notables attracts the attention of curators of manuscripts.

A fine point, useful as a time-saver: ask the curator of manuscripts for the names of other people who have recently done research in the same collections. Then ask those people if they can and will save you time by pinpointing items or dates that you need. Unless he looks on you as a direct competitor, another researcher is usually willing to cooperate in this way, knowing that you in turn may come across items that are helpful to him. Thus two scholars can be of mutual assistance.

Now See:
The National Archives (p. 109)

Publishing an Author's Query

In certain kinds of research, especially in biography, it can be useful for the researcher to make public his need for information, in the hope that volunteers will make contact with him. This is best done by publishing an author's query in several newspapers or scholarly journals best calculated to get results. A favorite literary vehicle is the letters column of *The New York Times Book Review*. In other parts of the country an author's query can well be placed in the letters column of the major metropolitan dailies.

The querying author (researcher) takes his chances on being overwhelmed with familiar material he neither needs nor wants. His best protection is to phrase the query so that its scope is plainly limited. It can specify that the writer is seeking "those with personal knowledge" of the subject, or "original letters and manuscripts." Even if no worthwhile information results from the published query, the time taken to publish it is minimal. But it may open entirely new avenues of research, particularly through interview, and lead directly to fresh sources of written material.

Obtaining Out-of-Print Books

There are situations in research work when you want to obtain your own copy of an out-of-print book (called an "o-p book" in the trade), one that you can no longer buy from an ordinary retail bookstore or direct from the publisher. This occurs when you need a book for reference over a long period, and it is inconvenient to consult a library copy on every occasion.

1. *Book-search specialists.* The best method to get your own copy is to use the services offered by a book-search specialist in the out-of-print book market. Some are connected with book shops; others work from their homes with no stock on hand. The expert book-finder is a vanishing species, but as long as some of them are around they will perform a service at reasonable cost that no amateur can hope to match. Their classified ads can be found in literary journals and in the book review sections of major newspapers such as *The New York Times*, the *Chicago Tribune* and the *Washington Post*. These specialists use an inexpensive communication network among their colleagues (including printed lists of books wanted), by which they can reach all the known out-of-print book dealers by mail or telephone. Your inquiry for a given title thus becomes known to a large circle of dealers. Those who can supply the book communicate with your dealer, who in turn notifies you. Practices vary, but in general o-p book dealers ask for payment in advance before mailing you the book. Reputable dealers rate the physical condition of each book as "excellent," "good," "fair," etc. and charge accordingly. All factors considered, I have found their prices very reasonable compared to the time and cost of doing the searching myself, without detailed knowledge of which specialists are most likely to have what I want.

2. *Out-of-print bookstores.* Researchers who live in cities big enough to support one or more out-of-print bookstores can go to the store and spend time looking for what they want on the shelves. They can also leave a book-search request with the store, provided it offers a book-search service. Prices of books which you locate in a store are likely to be lower than those obtained through the network of o-p dealers, so it sometimes saves money to hunt in a few stores yourself and save the service markup. However, many of the

grand old o-p bookstores are disappearing, like Lowdermilk's in Washington, and Leary's in Philadelphia, so this method becomes less practical as the years pass.

3. *University Microfilms International (UMI)*. A relatively new method of obtaining a copy of an out-of-print book is to have a copy (or copies) made to order. This service is offered by UMI through its Books On Demand program (for information call toll free 800-521-0600). UMI is a subsidiary of the Xerox Corporation and has all the dynamism of that great and exciting company. When it receives an inquiry for a xerographic or microfilm copy of a particular book, UMI first looks into its catalog of nearly 100,000 book titles already on film in its vault to see if that title is on hand. If so, the customer is quoted a price, which is based largely on the size of the book (average price in 1979 was about $30). If necessary, UMI can also draw on tens of thousands of other titles available through other divisions of the company, and through cooperating publishers who will lend UMI a rare book so that a negative can be made. The charge in this case is higher than for a book already on film.

Books are printed by the xerographic process on acid-free paper that holds up well. Books are bound in either paper or cloth as desired. The company pays royalties to the original publisher where necessary and ships the customer the bound book or microfilm roll. UMI offers discounts for multiple orders of the same title. At regular intervals it issues a catalog of o-p books that it holds in its microfilm vault.

4. *Reprints.* Watch for the long out-of-print title to reappear in a reprint edition. With the recent development of efficient, inexpensive photo-reproduction methods, which can replace costly typesetting, it has become economic for publishers to issue reprint editions in limited quantities. The reprint book industry has burgeoned since 1960, to the point where there are hundreds of reprint book publishers active in the United States. Many are specialists in subjects that have attracted great interest recently — such as black biography. Some are able to publish hard cover reprint editions profitably in quantities as low as 300–400 — about 10 percent of the number of copies required for profitability in normal publishing with its high typesetting costs. Tens of thousands of titles, once out of print, are now available from reprint publishers.

Once a reprint edition appears, a reference to it may be inserted (but not always) in *Books in Print*, published by R. R. Bowker (see p. 34), and the research worker may find it there. Another source for information on recent reprint titles is the annual *Guide to Reprints*, along with its companion *Subject Guide to Reprints*, which are international in scope and include more than 100,000 titles in several languages from more than 400 publishers. They are published by Reprint Distribution Services, Inc., P.O. Box 249, Kent, Connecticut 06757.

A somewhat dated list of U.S. reprint publishers is contained in *Scholarly Reprint Publishing in the United States*, a book by Carol A. Nemeyer, published in 1972 by R. R. Bowker.

Oral History Collections

A new kind of research resource has appeared since 1948 — the oral history collection. An oral history collection consists of tapes and typed transcripts of interviews recorded by trained interviewers with people having memories of important events or personalities. These interviews have added substantially to the written documentation of the recent past because they have tapped the knowledge of people who for one reason or another could not, or would not, take the time to write them down. One hour of skilled interviewing can result in a document of great research value that otherwise might never have been produced. This is particularly the case with information obtained from aged people, and from extremely busy people who are not used to writing. Oral history collections are most frequently projects of universities, libraries and historical societies. They concentrate on the memories and comments of prominent people, or on those with intimate knowledge of the prominent. There are special purpose collections, however, concentrating on the history of a locality, a company, an industry, or even an entire movement, like the civil rights movement.

Oral history in its modern form started in 1948 with the establishment of the Oral History Research Office of Columbia University, the biggest and best-known collection of this type, and has expanded rapidly in the United States and abroad. In 1971 the Columbia University group compiled and published for the Oral History Association (see below) a listing of all known oral history programs in the United States (*Oral History in the United States — a Directory*, compiled by Gary L. Shumway). This 120-page book describes the collections at more than 200 institutions, and lists more than 90 others where oral history collections were planned at the time of publication. In 1975 the R. R. Bowker Company published *Oral History Collections*, a guide to collections in 388 institutions. More recently the Oral History Association (see below) in collaboration with the American Library Association undertook to compile a new directory of oral history collections, scheduled for publication in 1981.

The Columbia Oral History Research Office (Box 20, Butler Library, Columbia University, New York, N.Y. 10027) keeps in print a descriptive catalog of its own holdings (nearly 4,000 persons interviewed through 1978, and roughly a half million pages of manuscript). It is edited by Louis M. Starr and Elizabeth B. Mason and will be found in most reference libraries. Columbia offers a research service for those unable to visit its collection, and it has pioneered in making oral history more accessible to researchers. In 1970 it reached an agreement with a subsidiary of *The New York Times*, Microfilming Corporation of America (1620 Hawkins Avenue, Sanford, N.C. 27330), to start reproducing its collection on microfilm and microfiche so that it can be shared with many libraries. More than 800 are available in this form. Microfilming Corporation of America now distributes copies of material in other collections as well as those at Columbia. Some memoirs which have been restricted by interviewees will become open to general use in the years ahead.

Early in 1968 oral historians from all parts of the United States established the Oral History Association (permanent address at Columbia University, above), which holds annual workshops and publishes a review as well as a newsletter. Cataloging of major collections was begun by the National Union Catalog of Manuscript Collections (see p. 103) in 1971.

New oral history projects are springing up all over the country. Progress in this field is so rapid that researchers should take care to check at every institution and library they use to find out: (1) whether an oral history program useful to them has been started there recently; and (2), whether it has, on film or paper, copies of material from the Columbia University collection, or any other. Many collections are indexed, and some have master indices, cross-referencing their entire oral history collections.

Specialized Sources of Information

There are so many specialized sources of information available to the thorough research worker that it would be futile to attempt to list them all. There is no substitute for remaining constantly alert to the possibility of fresh sources of which you may not yet have heard, but which are a familiar story to others. In addition, new information services are coming into being all the time, as man's need to know in detail becomes more pressing, and as the technology for recording, storing, retrieving, transmitting and duplicating information moves rapidly forward. Here are a few specialized sources among many:

1. *The National Archives.* This is the federal government agency in Washington, D.C., responsible for keeping the permanent records of the U.S. government. Its holdings include the original correspondence files and office records of all kinds of government officials, such as generals, Indian Commissioners and members of the President's Cabinet. The National Archives contains treaties, messages to Congress, U.S. Census records, maps, photographs, motion picture films, microfilms and sound recordings. The demarcation line between those original materials properly belonging in the National Archives and those belonging to the Library of Congress has not always been clear. Therefore researchers on a project related to government activity should check both places.

The National Archives is a part of the National Archives and Records Services (NARS), which in turn is part of the General Services Administration, Washington, D.C. 20408. NARS also administers the Presidential Libraries (located in home towns of several Presidents) containing collections of papers relating to all Presidents from Hoover to the present. A catalog of NARS publications can be obtained from the address above, or from the Government Printing Office (see p. 65).

2. *United Nations Publications.* Since its foundation the United Nations has published and placed on sale an increasing amount of documentation on a wide variety of subjects of public and international concern. U.N. material is produced in clothbound and paperbound books, pamphlets, periodicals and official records, both printed and in multilith form. Much of it is recurrent — in yearbooks or annual surveys, bulletins, series and annual reports. All are published in English, and in many cases they are available in French, Spanish and Russian. Catalogs of U.N. publications and information on what is available can be obtained from Dept. of Public Information, United Nations, New York, N.Y. 10017.

Subject categories of U.N. publications include, among others: cartography, economics, social questions, international law, transport and communications, atomic energy, narcotic drugs, demography, human rights, public finance, international statistics, and treaties. The publications of the intergovernmental agencies (commonly considered as related to the U.N.) are available through their own separate sales organizations, addresses of which can be obtained from the U.N. publications office (above). Some of these intergovernmental agencies are: the International Labor Organization; Food and Agriculture Organization; World Health Organization; International Monetary Fund; Universal Postal Union.

3. *State and City Government Agencies.* In following every research question for which the answer, or part of the answer, may lie with an agency of state or local government, the same steps can be taken as have been recommended in this book for federal government. Printed documentation may not be so thorough as in federal government, because Washington has much more money for publications. Nevertheless, you should cover state and local government sources to find what you can. This means looking for annual reports of the governor and his department heads; checking the proceedings of the state legislature, as well as hearings and reports of committees of the legislature; asking the state government librarian and the director of the state archives what documents are open to researchers; and doing likewise, according to your project, with county and city officials and their records.

At the lower levels of government petty officials are often not used to dealing with scholars, but they are accustomed to inquiries from the press, from administrative officials and from legislators. If you should encounter officious obstruction by a low-rank public servant, show him a letter backing your research project signed by someone whose rank he respects.

4. *University Microfilms International (UMI)*

See First:
References to *University Microfilms International* on pp. 99 and 101

Because of the speed and thoroughness with which it is putting new technology to use in forms of interest to the researcher, this subsidiary of the Xerox Corporation warrants separate consideration as an information source. UMI offers such a variety of services in the microfilm and reprint fields that it is worthwhile for the serious investigator to obtain its full line of catalogs to see whether it has recently added a service that was not offered last year. UMI is at 300 North Zeeb Road, Ann Arbor, Mich. 48106.

Classification Systems Can Help You

If you learn something about the way libraries classify their books, and if you gain access to the stacks, you will find the books you need more quickly and easily. Whatever system your reference library may use (Dewey Decimal, Library of Congress, or any other), you should learn at the outset what system it employs. Second, you should ask for whatever printed guide or list is at hand that is used by the librarians to classify their newly acquired books. Such a list can steer you to books on the subjects you want to cover.

In libraries using the Library of Congress system, ask for the LC book entitled *Subject Headings Used in the Dictionary Catalog of the Library of Congress*. This is a detailed index to the call numbers (consisting of letters *and* numbers) under which books on given subjects are classified according to the LC system. For example, it shows that books about *Negro inventors* are classified under E185.8; books on *Executions and executioners* are classified under HV8551-3. On the way you have found out that at least some books have been written on these subjects (a fact of which you may not have been certain before consulting *Subject Headings*), otherwise the LC would not have assigned a classification number to them.

The next step is to ask the librarian for the *Library of Congress Classification Schedules*. These are a set of about thirty paperbound books and booklets, each of which outlines the subclassifications under a given initial letter, two initial letters, or subdivisions of one. Examples: H for sociology, L for education, M for music, T for technology. By studying the subclassifications adjoining the first one you sought, you may see others worth your attention. For example, close to the entry *Executions and executioners* (HV8551-3) you may find other interesting entries under *Crimes and offenses* (HV6251-7220), or *Prisons* (starting with HV8301).

If your work is concentrated in one area covered by one of these classification schedules, you might save time by purchasing it from the GPO (see p. 64). A free pamphlet entitled *Outline of Library of Congress Classification* is a helpful general aid, which can be obtained from the LC or from your Congressman.

Now See:
    Access to Library Stacks (p. 47)
    Your Congressman Can Help (p. 68)
    Buying Library of Congress Catalog Cards (p. 98)

Services from Periodicals

See First:
   Readers' Guide to Periodical Literature (p. 28)
   Periodical Indexes: the Two Levels (p. 29)
   Search Out the Trade Press (p. 89)

Periodicals, especially magazines with a long history of excellence in their specialties, sometimes provide services to the research worker that cannot be obtained elsewhere. Whether a given periodical will help you depends on the seriousness with which the staff takes your query, and the time and resources available. Frequently an inquiry from a subscriber or a "constant reader" will elicit an attempt to be helpful, because this is considered part of the magazine's public relations effort.

Back issues, as long as they last, are frequently supplied for nominal prices to those who write for them. *Tearsheets* of specified articles or pages, or facsimile copies of them, are often supplied free. Scientific journals print extra copies of articles routinely to supply to those who write to the journal requesting them. And frequently the author of the article, who is not on the staff of the periodical, will have a supply of reprints for distribution on request.

Another service, requiring more time of the magazine staff, is a search of the office index of the periodical in order to respond to a specific query. For instance, the magazine might be asked for references to back published material in more detail than the researcher could get from the relevant H. W. Wilson Co. index. The chances are excellent that the magazine maintains its own cumulated office index in much finer detail than Wilson does, because Wilson must cover hundreds of periodicals, and publishes its references for each year in separate volumes. One example: the National Geographic Society in Washington, D.C., maintains an excellent card index of every article, important subject and picture that has appeared in the *National Geographic Magazine* over many years.

Several decades ago it was normal for many American magazines to print an annual index. You can find these in bound library volumes of magazines dated in the 1920s and earlier. But with the rise of the several periodical indexes published by H. W. Wilson Co. this practice has largely disappeared from American periodical publishing.

Beyond the Written Word: Multimedia Sources

See First:
Know the Reference Book Catalogs (p. 49)

The last few years have seen a rapid expansion in the production and use of films, filmstrips, slides, tapes and transparencies as means of communication and instruction. To a great extent they have been produced as educational materials, the primary sales target being the schools. They have also been produced as training aids for organizations in business and for government-related agencies, such as the military. And they have been produced and circulated for public relations and sales purposes. In addition, tapes of programs originating with radio and television stations are at times available for rental or sale. All of these non-print forms of communication can have value for the individual doing research, because one can often learn from them things that print cannot convey.

How can the researcher go about finding whatever materials of this type there may be that are relevant to his inquiry? The catalog of the R. R. Bowker Company (see p. 49) is a rich source of information on specialized directories in this field, and the researcher can best examine it for himself. Particularly noteworthy is *Audiovisual Market Place: A Multimedia Guide*, which is kept up to date with regular new editions. It helps the user locate more than 5,000 firms and individuals now active in providing audiovisual goods and services in all parts of the country. There are other helpful Bowker publications listed in its catalog under art, graphics, education, films and other headings — too many to detail here.

One should not overlook the possibility that special libraries, and the headquarters of associations, have all kinds of non-print materials that they have collected on a casual basis. A company library or its public relations office, for example, may not have intended to make a collection, but it may have become the repository for such things as a tape recording of the remarks made at the retirement dinner for an outgoing president; informal photos of company events intended for a house organ; or home movies made by a company officer showing his colleagues at play, and turned over to the company by his survivors. It is therefore worthwhile to ask about such informally collected items that might not normally be listed in a library's catalog of holdings.

Keeping Alert to New Technology

See First:
Beyond the Written Word: Multimedia Sources (p. 113)

Since the mid-1960s, new information technology has been developed and put to use at an increasingly rapid rate. For instance, there has been miniaturization, first in the form of microfilm reels; then on microfiche, which are 4" × 6" film cards reproducing about 60 standard pages; and more recently on *ultramicrofiche*, which can hold up to 3,000 pages on one 4" × 6" film card (35 rows of tiny pictures, each with 85 pages). There are combination viewer-printers which enlarge a filmed page for viewing on a screen, and can then produce a paper copy of the page being shown. There are distance duplicating systems by which a paper copy can be produced in one city from an original placed into the duplicating-transmission equipment in another city. There are thousands of computer-based banks of data, such as company personnel records, the details of which are known only to the few people responsible for using them. And there are computerized information systems that print out, on command, all kinds of information ranging from short bibliographies to lengthy series of article abstracts.

Many reference librarians and university scholars whose degrees were obtained before such innovations are not fully aware of some of the new fact-finding methods this technology has made possible. They therefore cannot always guide students and other researchers in their use. Nor is there a foolproof method for keeping abreast of all new research resources. The best we can do is to remain constantly alert to the fact that new resources are appearing all the time. We should not hesitate to ask at companies, libraries, public agencies, publishers, etc. what new services they may have added lately, and what they know about what neighboring organizations have added.

A good general source of information in this field is the Information Industry Association (316 Pennsylvania Ave., S.E., Washington, D.C. 20003; telephone 202-544-1969). This is the trade association of private, for-profit information companies in the United States. The IIA was organized in November 1968 by a group of twenty companies involved with new forms of information technology and services, and it has since grown to embrace a membership of more than 125 companies. The IIA publishes a newsletter, and holds periodic conferences on information industry issues. The IIA staff under President Paul Zurkowski answers mail queries relating directly to information services provided by its members.

Two magazines can be particularly helpful to anyone who wants to keep up with products of the new technology that are being offered to libraries. *Special Libraries*, the monthly organ of the Special Libraries Association, is rich with advertising that explains newly available products that serve the purposes of special libraries, and thus of their clientele. The articles in *Special Libraries* are written primarily for librarians, but the researcher who looks over their shoulder at their own trade journal may learn about new tools to help him find facts faster.

Similarly, a relatively new quarterly, *Microform Review*, can help the researcher keep abreast of developments in microform technology and, especially through the advertisements, find out which companies are offering what new products and services. The magazine publisher itself issues the *Guide to Microforms in Print*, which can help the researcher find material that has not been reprinted in book form, but which is available in microform. The address of *Microform Review:* P.O. Box 405, Saugatuck Station, Westport, Connecticut 06880.

Computer-based information banks are all around us these days. One of the best known among librarians and the public is The Information Bank, a subsidiary of The New York Times Company. This is a telephone-access system which supplies the customer with a printout on his terminal of abstracts of articles from *The New York Times* and a large number of other periodicals whose contents are stored in The Information Bank. The customer must be specially trained to send in queries correctly from his keyboard. Service charges are based on the time during which the customer is connected to The Information Bank, both to transmit queries and to receive printout answers. Other examples of such services, both requiring operator training, are ORBIT, of the System Development Corporation, and DIALOG Information Retrieval Service, operated by Lockheed.

These are time-saving devices that can produce a huge collection of references very quickly. The individual researcher may be able to draw on them if he has the right connection with a paying customer. But they all rest on the research and indexing skill of the people behind the scenes who compiled the references in the first place, following the research principles outlined in this book. If the human being who did the original research overlooked a few references, the electronic machine will not produce them.

For the researcher the art in using computer-based information systems lies first in finding out what organizations have stored in computers data that he can use; and second, in getting permission, or authority, to retrieve the data, if any is there. Of course, there have for some years been organizations which have compiled specialized information in computers, particularly in the natural sciences, and have supplied customers with printouts according to their specifications. A pharmaceutical manufacturer, for example, might request a list of all scientific journal articles containing the words "heart" or "blood" in the title, and such a list is easily produced.

A critical point for the computer as a research instrument, just as in the standard written indexes of books and periodicals, is in the accuracy of the indexer. An error at the coding stage can, in fact, be even more damaging in a computer than in traditional written form, because the error on magnetic tape is more difficult to detect. Therefore, the research worker should look on the computer as a time-saving electronic file, but not as a "brain" or as an instrument that will replace his own powers to observe and to think. The computer is, after all, an amazingly fast-working, obedient, automatic idiot. As far as we can see ahead, it will never possess the inspiration or the critical faculties of man.

Index

About the Author

Alden Todd is the author of five previous books: *Abandoned: The Story of the Greely Arctic Expedition; Justice on Trial: The Case of Louis D. Brandeis; A Spark Lighted in Portland; Richard Montgomery, Rebel of 1775*, and *Favorite Subjects in Western Art* (with Dorothy B. Weisbord). He has edited other books and written numerous national magazine articles.

Since 1968 he has been an editor and publications director of Deloitte Haskins & Sells, the international public accounting firm. He has been an officer of the American Society of Journalists and Authors, and is a member of the Industrial Communication Council and the Authors Guild of America. Since 1966 he has taught the course in Research Techniques and Fact-Finding at the New York University School of Continuing Education.

Notes

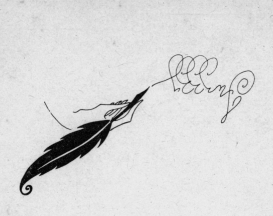